IMAGES OF W

MONTE CASSINO

A US Sherman of Company B, 760th Tank Battalion bogged down in a creek on 12 May 1944, showing the difficulties armour faced in the terrain around Monte Cassino. (NARA)

IMAGES OF WAR

MONTE CASSINO

ARMOURED FORCES IN THE BATTLE FOR THE GUSTAV LINE

RARE PHOTOGRAPHS FROM WARTIME ARCHIVES

Jeffrey Plowman

Pen & Sword
MILITARY

First published in Great Britain in 2018 by
PEN & SWORD MILITARY
an imprint of
Pen & Sword Books Ltd,
47 Church Street,
Barnsley,
South Yorkshire
S70 2AS

ISBN 978 1 52671 893 8

Typeset by CHIC GRAPHICS

Printed and bound by CPI Group (UK) Ltd, Croydon, CR0 4YY

Pen & Sword Aviation, Pen & Sword Family History, Pen & Sword Maritime, Pen &
Sword Military, Pen & Sword Discovery, Wharncliffe Local History, Wharncliffe True
Crime, Wharncliffe Transport, Pen and Sword Select, Pen and Sword Military Classics,
Leo Cooper, The Praetorian Press, Remember When, Seaforth Publishing and
Frontline Publishing.

For a complete list of Pen & Sword titles please contact
Pen & Sword Books Limited
47 Church Street, Barnsley, South Yorkshire, S70 2AS, England
E-mail: enquiries@pen-and-sword.co.uk
Website: www.pen-and-sword.co.uk

Contents

Introduction

To any visitor to Italy today Monte Cassino and its Benedictine monastery is an imposing sight. This mountain, some 520m high, and those of the Arunci mountains across the Liri valley were a formidable bulwark against the Allied drive on the road to Rome. In fact the Italian Military College had long regarded Monte Cassino as an example of an impregnable natural defensive position and used it for many years as the basis of an exercise for their staff corps officers. Thus when it came to establishing their defences in Italy in 1943 the Germans showed no hesitation in incorporating the Cassino massif into what was to become the Gustav Line. In the end it would take the Allies some five months to achieve a breakthrough, their fourth and final assault being launched in May 1944. Ironically, this they achieved not by capturing Monte Cassino itself but by breaking through on the opposite side of the valley in the Arunci mountains.

Monte Cassino and the Benedictine monastery atop it presented a formidable sight to any attacking forces as this view from American positions at the entrance to the Liri Valley attests. (NARA)

While Italy was hardly ideal country for armoured operations, even the plains of the Po having their limitations, armour was essential to the Allies as much as it was for its German defenders. In fact the Italian terrain, dotted with its numerous villages, proved ideal for employing tanks in defensive operations, particularly when Panthers and Tigers appeared on the scene. Thus, while the battle for Cassino was primarily an infantry one, especially early on, armour did have its part to play in the fighting.

While there have been many books written on the fighting at Cassino, not many have focused on the role armour had to play in it. Thus this book is an attempt to redress this aspect of the fighting around Cassino.

On 26 November 1943 an Allied reconnaissance aircraft took this oblique aerial photograph of Cassino township providing the best image of the town before it was almost totally destroyed in 1944. (Geoffrey Duff)

Photographic Sources

I wish to thank the following for photographs and information: Lee Archer, Peter Brown, Terry Brown, Wojciech Gawyrich, Daniele Guglielmi, Wolfgang Loof, Karlheinz Muench and Zbigniew Lalak.

I am grateful to the following veterans and families of veterans for making their photographs available over the years: George Andrews, Frank Bulling, Frank J. Davis, Geoffrey Duff, Rod Eastgate, Jim Furness, Pat Gourdie, Frank Harvey, Shirley Hodson, Harry Hopping, Pierre Ichac, Jim Moodie, Stratton Morrin, Georg Schmitz and Stuart Wilson.

I am also grateful to the following archives and organizations for making photographs available to me: the Alexander Turnbull Library (ATL) New Zealand, the Imperial War Museum (IWM), the Médiathèque de la Défense, d' Ivry (ECPAD), the National Army Museum of New Zealand (NAMNZ), the US National Archives and Records Service (NARA) and the Polish Institute and Sikorski Museum (PISM).

Chapter One

The Road to Cassino

On the morning of 15 January 1944, after a long struggle up the peninsula from Salerno, the Americans finally took Monte Trocchio. From summit of this peak the broad flat valley of the Liri River appeared to stretch for miles and it must have seemed to them that they only had to cross the swift Gari River below and the road to Rome was theirs. Sadly this did not prove to be the case. Instead they were facing one of the strongest German defensive positions in Italy, the Gustav Line, thanks to Generalfeldmarschall Albert Kesselring, Commander-in-Chief of Heeresgruppe C in Italy. Unwilling to give up southern Italy so easily, he had managed to convince Adolf Hitler that this was the right strategy and had set up a series of defensive lines across the peninsula, the first of which, the Barbara Line, the Allies had already encountered. The Gustav Line ran along the lower reaches of the Garigliano River to Monte Cassino and because of the strategic importance of the Liri Valley was one that the Germans had put considerable effort into its development.

Just why the Allies invaded Italy in the first place is another matter. The Americans had been against a campaign in what the British Prime Minister, Winston Churchill, termed the 'soft underbelly of Europe'. Their eyes had always been set on a cross-Channel invasion of France from England. The problem for the Americans was that at the time of their entry into the war they lacked the resources, both in men and materiel, to pursue this aim. Thus they had no choice but to enter the Mediterranean theatre of operations, first in North Africa in support of the British and then in the invasion of Sicily. Neither of these operations were particularly desirable to the Americans but the seizure of the latter did offer the possibility of an alternative route into France, via Sardinia and Corsica.

However, fate intervened after they landed on Sicily, bringing with it a new and unexpected opportunity as it led to the collapse of the regime of the Italian dictator Benito Mussolini. Lacking the courage to continue the war, the new Italian government then entered into secret negotiations with the Allies that ultimately led to an agreement for the Italian armed forces to lay down their arms. The Germans, on hearing of the announcement of the armistice between the Allies and Italy, had moved rapidly to take over the country. In the north Generalfeldmarschall Erwin

Rommel's Heersgruppe B seized the main centres there and disarmed the Italian troops under his command. In the south the Germans had actually intended to withdraw northwards after disarming the Italians, that is until Kesselring successfully argued against this plan. This was partly driven by the impracticality of pulling his troops out without losing too much in the way of men and materiel but also because of the importance of the airfields around Foggia. Instead, after disarming the Italian troops under his command, Kesselring began the construction of a series of defensive lines across the Italian peninsula.

Having had their hands forced the Americans reluctantly agreed to landings on the Italian mainland but only on the understanding that it would help tie down German forces in Italy and secure the airfields around Foggia, the latter for use by their bombers against mainland Europe. The first of these were made in the toe of the peninsula, at Reggio di Calabria, by General Sir Bernard Montgomery's 8th Army but their progress was slow. These were soon followed by the main assault in the Bay of Salerno by General Mark W. Clark's US 5th Army on 3 September 1943, then later by landings of British airborne troops at Taranto. The main force at Salerno soon ran into trouble when they encountered bitter opposition as they began to fight their way off the beaches. At one point the German assault threatened to throw them back into the sea. Ironically, more success was had on the Adriatic coast where the British paratroopers, despite the lack of transport, heavy weapons and armour, managed to secure Bari and Brindisi before the area was sealed off by what German troops there were in the region. Eventually the situation at Salerno stabilized and the Allies were free to expand. British troops entered Naples on 1 October, Foggia on the Adriatic falling to paratroopers the same day.

Unfortunately, the lack of a cohesive strategy by the Allies in the Mediterranean started to work against them. With winter fast approaching, the question arose as to what to do next. Given that their principal aims had been to eliminate Italy from the war and tie down the maximum number of German units there, the Allies had succeeded admirably in the first instance. The trouble was that the second was so vague as to be absolutely meaningless. Having secured the vital ports and airfields in the south of the peninsula there was a feeling that they had gained enough to give their naval and air forces control of the southern Adriatic and Ionian seas. On the other hand, though pushing north would give them the access to airfields around Rome, they saw no advantage in areas beyond there. Nevertheless, their successes up to that point had given them hope that an occupation up to the Northern Appenines was possible. There were even advantages to be gained by pushing beyond there and into the plains of the Po River. At their Quadrant Conference in Quebec a general agreement was reached that, while progress in

Italy was likely to be slow, Rome was an important objective that should be seized as soon as possible.

At the strategic conference at Teheran at the end of November between Churchill and his Allied counterparts, President Franklin D. Roosevelt of the USA and Josef Stalin of the USSR, an agreement was eventually reached to continue the offensive in Italy. This was despite misgivings on the part of Stalin that the British and Americans had designs on Europe east of Italy. While the main focus of the Americans was in the invasion of northwest Europe, they did agree to a landing in southern France. This in turn strengthened their desire to secure Rome and, in fact, to be well north of it by the spring of 1944 as their intention was to launch their assault on southern France from northern Italy. Thus, whether the Americans liked it or not, they were being drawn deeper into the mire that was to become the Italian campaign.

Before that could happen they needed to secure their hold on Naples and Foggia by establishing a line along the Volturno and Biferno Rivers. Clark's troops ran up against the former on 6 October, a day before the 8th Army secured Termoli on the Biferno. From here on the British 8th Army found themselves in some tactically ugly terrain where the plains around Foggia gave way to hills cut by rivers running down to the sea.

Things were no better on the other side of the Apennines, as north of the Volturno River the Americans found themselves up against 40 miles of mountainous terrain before they could draw up against the Bernhardt Line along the line of the Garigliano River. Worst still the autumn rains had struck in their full fury, turning the river flats into a sea of mud. In the end Clark's attack over the Volturno was not launched until 12 October. This forced the Germans to retreat towards their next defensive position, the Barbara Line, the Allies reaching this on 2 November. By early November this too had been breached, the Germans falling back to the Bernhardt Line.

On the Adriatic coast the British 8th Army had to pause along the line of the Trigno River in order to re-group and reorganize their logistics thanks to the poor roads they had to operate over. As a result they were not able to launch their attack until 2 November. However, a day later they had penetrated three miles beyond it, leaving the Germans with no choice but to fall back to the line of the Sangro River. This the 8th Army's forward elements reached on 9 November.

Back on the Tyrrhenian side of the Apennines and to the north of the Barbara Line the Americans found that the coastal plain was beset by marshes leaving them the only realistic path to the Liri valley along Route 6 through the Mignano Gap. This area was the responsibility of 10 Armee under the command of Generaloberst Heinrich-Gottfried von Vietinghoff-Scheel. Further north defence of the Cassino sector fell to Generalleutnant Fridolin von Senger und Etterlin's XIV Panzerkorps.

The US 5th Army finally launched its assault on the mountains around the Mignano Gap on 1 December, but the weather ultimately proved their undoing. Fighting continuing until the end of the year when a blizzard forced them to halt their attack, reorganize and replace their losses. Their final offensive to clear the Germans east of the Garigliano was launched on 4 January, ending eleven days later after the Germans withdrew across the river.

Several days later the Corps Expéditionaire Français (CEF), under Général Alphonse Juin, struck out for Sant'Elia from their positions in the mountains to the north of the US 5th Army. Advancing through the mountains they soon found a gap in the German defences to the south of Acquafondata. In the resulting fighting the German mountain troops suffered heavily and to avoid being wiped out were forced to conduct a fighting withdrawal. Pressing home their advantage, the French troops pushed on until they had taken all their objectives. The last, Sant'Elia, was secured on 16 January after being abandoned by the Germans.

The next phase of the advance of the 5th Army called for them to break into the western end of the German Winter Line at Cassino and drive up the Liri Valley. At the same time, on the Adriatic coast, the British 8th Army had been tasked with securing Pescara and from there to swing south-west towards Avezzano with the aim of threatening the German lines of communication. To achieve this 2nd New Zealand Division, who had entered the Italian campaign for the first time, launched their assault across the Sangro River on 18 November. From there they easily took the heights above the river but failed to secure the next ridge, and the town of Orsogna, despite making three assaults. Further east on the coast the Canadians reached the town of Ortona on 20 December, finally taking it after eight days of intense house-to-house fighting against Fallschirmjäger-Regiment 3. However, by now the 8th Army's offensive had ground to a halt, with no chance of it resuming until the spring.

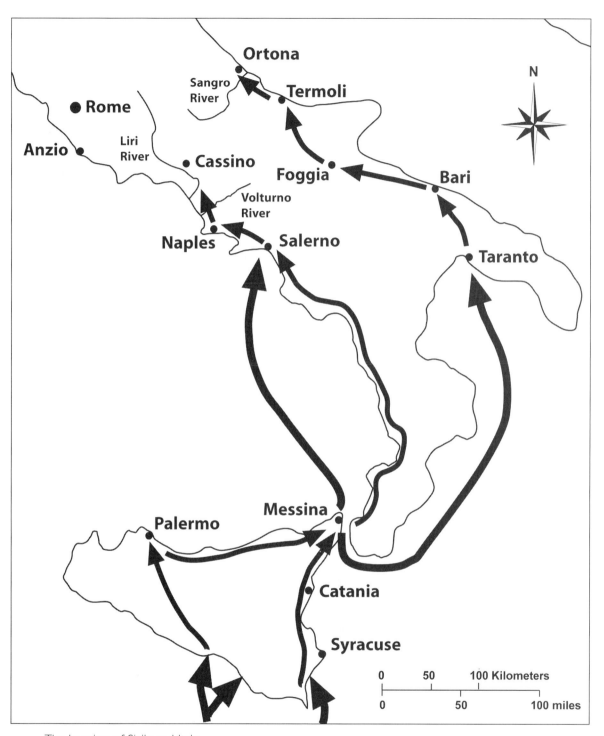

The Invasion of Sicily and Italy.

An American soldier inspects a knocked-out StuG III from the Panzer-Division Hermann Göring on Route 6 near San Vittore on 9 January 1944. (NARA)

On 13 January the 3éme Regiment de Spahis Algériens, under the command of Capitaine Henri Spandenberger, entered Acquafondata, part of the column halting in the town itself. (ECPAD)

The rest of the column, including this M5A1 Stuart tank, carried on beyond Acquafondata and halted at this hairpin bend. (ECPAD)

Another M5A1 Stuart tank from the 3éme Regiment de Spahis Algériens was photographed near Acquafondata. (ECPAD)

This M5A1 Stuart tank was photographed just beyond the hairpin bend. (ECPAD)

Chapter Two

Early Attacks on the Gustav Line

By the end of December 1943 it had become apparent to the Allies that the right hook on the Adriatic coast had failed and if they wanted to reach Rome by June 1944, their only option was an attack up the Liri Valley but there were constraints on this. One of their strategies of opening this door involved a seaborne invasion behind German lines in the Anzio-Nettuno area, codenamed Shingle. This needed to take place before the end of January 1944, as the landing craft and ships required for this would then be withdrawn in readiness for the assault on northern France. As it turned out this ultimately led to the Allies becoming enslaved to the needs of Shingle, initially simply to draw Axis troops south but after the launch of Shingle to break through to the beleaguered troops around Anzio. There were, however, times when their operations seemed to be driven by the need to keep pressure on the Germans in the south to prevent their transfer north to Anzio. One thing the Allies could not stop was the transfer of German troops from the Adriatic coast to the American 5th Army front after it became apparent that Allied operations on the Adriatic were showing signs of winding down, 26 Panzer-Division being the first to go. What the Allies were now facing at the entrance to the Liri Valley was perhaps one of their most formidable German defensive positions in Italy. This was the Gustav Line, a string of defences that coincided with the Bernhardt Line along the lower reaches of the Garigliano but which turned northwards through the Arunci Mountains before passing through Monte Cassino itself.

With Operation Shingle timed to start on 22 January the Allies began their diversionary operations further south in what turned out to be a piecemeal operation. The British, having reached the Bernhardt and Gustav Lines first, began their assault over the lower Garigliano River on the night of 17/18 January. Codenamed Operation Panther, it had mixed results. The leading troops of 56th Division managed to cross successfully, though many of their assault boats were lost in the process. The following morning they were reinforced by more infantry and anti-tank guns, while a few tanks from 23rd Armoured Brigade caught up with them around midday. However, things did not go as well for 5th Division on their right, some of their infantry being held up by minefields on the other side or forced to switch their crossing point. Further south the units sent around the coast became dispersed across their landing areas, while the landing craft carrying their supporting tanks were forced to return to base because of incorrectly-placed landing marks.

The Germans were quick to respond and on 19 January the leading elements of 5th Division came under a strong counter-attack from Panzer-Regiment Herman Göring though this was eventually repulsed. After learning of this Kesselring despatched further elements of the Herman Göring Panzer Division and a regiment from 94 Infanterie-Division. He also sent 29 Panzergrenadier-Division to the area around Esperia-Ausonia but this was not enough to prevent the British taking both Tufo and Minturno. Their successes there and elsewhere forced Kesselring into committing 29 Panzergrenadier-Division and this deployment prevented Castelforte falling into British hands. Nevertheless further gains were made over the next few days by the British forces, the fighting reaching its crescendo on 21 January. By now, however, with both sides throwing more troops into the British bridgehead, the situation was rapidly approaching a stalemate situation the Allies finally calling off the offensive on 9 February and drawing off troops to send to Anzio.

Operation Panther was supposed to reach its peak around the time 36th Texan Division launched its assault over the Gari River and this was to be coordinated with another attack by the British 46th Division around the confluence of the Garigliano, Gari and Liri Rivers on the night of 19/20 January. Unfortunately this attack failed miserably. Just before the assault began the Germans opened the sluice gates of a dam further up the Liri Valley turning the river into a raging torrent. As a result very few of the British assault troops managed to cross the Garigliano. Those that did were soon rounded up and taken prisoner and no further attempt was made by them to cross the river, much to the annoyance of the Americans.

The Texans had no better luck. They launched their assault either side of Sant'Angelo in Theodice on the night of 20/21 January but experienced problems crossing the rapidly-flowing Gari River. Many of their assault boats capsized as soon as they climbed into them, while others were holed by bullet on the way forward and sank halfway across the river. Their engineers attempted to establish footbridges over the river but at least one was defective, another was destroyed on the way up, while a third was established but concentration of shellfire forced its abandonment. An effort was made to push over Bailey bridges over but the engineers had to give up after coming under intensive German fire. Nevertheless, the Texans managed to get some troops across but the arrival of daylight brought a halt to any further crossings and those troops that had crossed soon became isolated and taken prisoner. A second attempt to cross the Gari was made the following night and though several battalions succeeded they became isolated and resistance soon

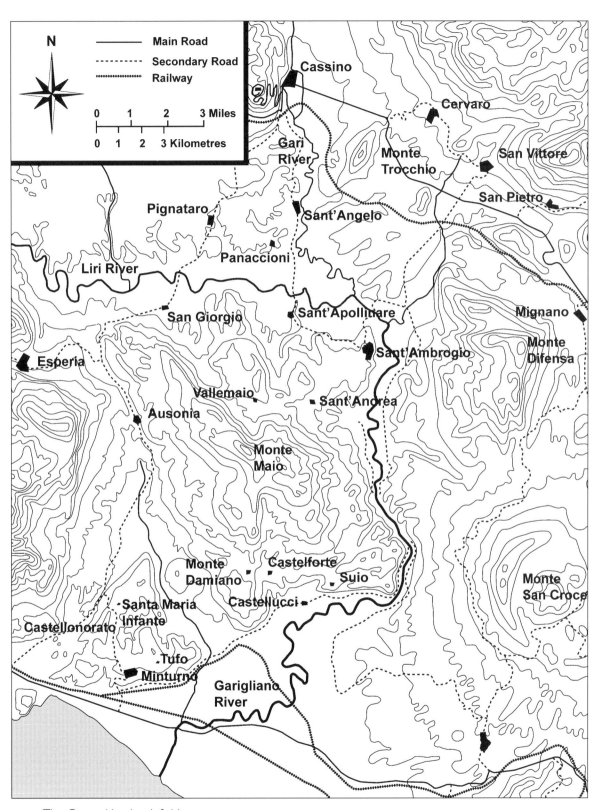

Cassino

Cervaro

San Vittore

Gari River

Monte Trocchio

San Pietro

Pignataro

Sant'Angelo

Panaccioni

Mignano

Liri River

San Giorgio

Sant'Apollinare

Monte Difensa

Esperia

Sant'Ambrogio

Vallemaio

Sant'Andrea

Ausonia

Monte Maio

Castelforte

Monte Damiano

Suio

Monte San Croce

Castellucci

Santa Maria Infante

Castellonorato

Tufo

Minturno

Garigliano River

The Gustav Line battlefield.

ceased. In the end the Texans abandoned their assault, having suffered some 1,681 casualties.

Despite all of this effort Shingle, launched on the night of 22 January, failed miserably. The Anzio landings themselves were unopposed and the troops had no trouble establishing a perimeter its commander Major General John P. Lucas failed to exploit that and instead put his efforts into consolidating his position. In the meantime Kesselring rushed every available unit he had to the area and within three days had established a ring around the bridgehead, while the German artillery had a clear view from the hills and mountains above it. Worst still another more troops were on their way. At the end of January, before these reinforcements arrived, Lucas launched a two-pronged attack but by this time the Germans were in a strong position and no real progress was made.

The final move at Cassino was made on 25 January when the CEF were diverted from their thrust towards Atina to launch assaults on Colle Abate, Colle Belvedere and the village of Terelle to the north of Cassino township. After some intense fighting they secured both Abate and Belvedere only to come under an intense series of counter-attacks. The most serious of these saw them driven off the summit of Belvedere and cut off, some without food and water for three days, until relieved. The Germans, having shot their bolt, were eventually forced to withdraw leaving the French to consolidate their hold on both peaks.

Though the first tanks were sent over the Garigliano River on 18 January, reinforcements were sent over later, such as this M4A2 Sherman from 40th Royal Tank Regiment on 20 January. (IWM)

Among the tanks lost by 40th Royal Tank Regiment was this M4A2 Sherman, seen here on this bridge on the Suio road near the town of San Lorenzo. (NARA)

Chapter Three

The First Battle

With the Texan Division's attack a failure, the Americans turned their attention to the town of Cassino and Monte Cassino. This task was assigned to Major General Charles W. Ryder's 34th Division, backed up by Shermans from Colonel Harry W. Sweeting's 756th Tank Battalion. Facing them in Cassino were Generalleutnant Franek's 44 Grenadier-Division, with Grenadier-Regiment 211 from 71 Infanterie-Division, many occupying reinforced shelters in the ground floors or basements of buildings in the town. For armoured support they had some Sturmgeschütz IIIs assault guns from Sturmgeschütz-Abteilung 242.

When the attack kicked off on the night of 24/25 January the infantry ran into trouble almost from the start. The Germans had blown a bridge to the west of Caira, resulting the diversion of the Rapido River into a series of irrigation canals on the eastern bank, in the process turning the ground into a morass. The leading battalion from 133rd Infantry Regiment, tasked with taking Monte Castellone, soon became caught up on the barbed wire and mines on the east bank of the Rapido River where they were cut to pieces by machine-gun fire. To their left Japanese-American troops from 100th Nisei Battalion, troops of the Hawaiian National Guard, were forced to dive into the irrigation ditches or simply dig in after the wind changed and blew away their covering smoke. In the end only three officers and eleven men reached the river, where they were forced to take cover in the dry riverbed. Those that attempted to scale the far bank ran into more barbed wire entanglements from which the Germans had hung booby traps. They were cut down by machine-gun fire. Some tanks attempted to move up but six become stuck in the boggy ground. Nevertheless, as the day wore on a few infantrymen from the assaulting battalions managed to cross the river and by nightfall had established a bridgehead on the other side. One of the battalions reached the base of Point 213 until fire from the Italian barracks drove them back. Another battalion got as far as the outskirts of Cassino but fire brought their advance to an end. Ryder ordered them back to the riverbed. Then, with covering fire from some tanks, they and 100th Nisei Battalion attacked Point 225 but were driven off.

Another attempt to force the river was made on 27 January with the view to eliminating the Germans to the northwest of the barracks on Point 213. This attack

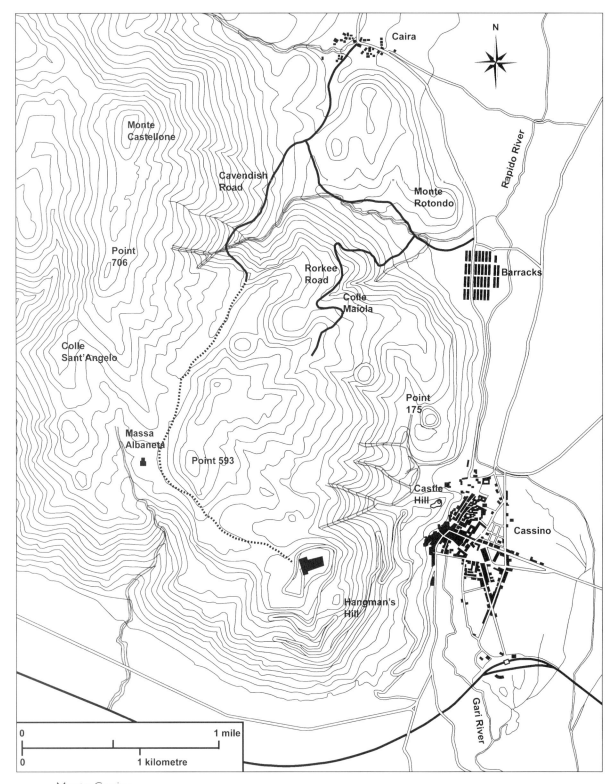

Monte Cassino.

was to be preceded by tanks, with Lieutenant Wayne B. Henry's 2nd Platoon detailed to support the crossing of the other tanks by direct fire. Unfortunately it did not start well. The assaulting platoon of tanks got onto the wrong road until Company B's commander, Captain Charles M. Wilkinson, redirected it. Shortly afterwards Wilkinson's tank became bogged when he drove off the road to avoid cutting a telephone line. Henry's tank ran into a lake of mud, forcing him to take over Sergeant Crawford's tank. Shortly afterwards Henry discovered a causeway on the other side of a water-filled ditch and beyond it a narrow bridge over the Rapido and with his other two tanks crossed the river. Once over they proceeded to clear away the anti-personnel mines and barbed wire that the Germans had laid in front of the American positions.

Next to cross was 3rd Platoon but Wilkinson discovered that their tanks had stopped moving forward. When he went to investigate he found that the platoon leader's tank had got stuck in the same water-filled ditch that Henry's platoon had successfully crossed, thus blocking that route. Wilkinson located an alternative route to the bridge over the Rapido, took over Sergeant Robert Osganian's tank and set off to the river, joining Henry's platoon. Once over the river Wilkinson destroyed a house in no man's land that had a machine-gun position built into the basement. Then all the tanks turned their attention to some houses at the base of the hills, before swinging southwards towards the barracks but without infantry support, the latter being slow to follow up. Shortly afterwards Sergeant Louis J. Jarvis' and Sergeant Roland L. Buys' tanks had to turn back as they were out of ammunition. Jarvis' tank backed onto a mine that the Germans had laid behind them, the explosion blowing off one of the tracks of his tank. He and his crew bailed out and crawled back along the trail left by their tank's tracks till they were out of the minefield. Buys attempted to get back across the Rapido but his tank got hung up on a ditch. When he climbed out to assess the situation his tank came under heavy fire and he was severely wounded. Wilkinson ordered Henry to get out as well but while backing out one track of Henry's tanks slipped off a bridge. Henry got out of the turret to investigate but was killed by a burst of machine-gun fire. Wilkinson, in the meantime, continued southwards, destroying a pillbox, only for his tank to be knocked out in turn by a panzerfaust that set it on fire. Both he and his crew and Henry's crew were captured.

Despite the loss of these tanks some infantry from 168th Infantry Regiment managed to reach the base of Point 213 around dusk, while another company made it to the summit that night. But their stay was short-lived. Realizing that their position would become untenable in the morning, their commander ordered them back across the river. On seeing this two other company commanders thought a general withdrawal was taking place and pulled their troops back over the river as well. This still left two companies on the west bank, so they were ordered to conform with the other companies, only to be sent 500 yards to the north where they re-crossed the river and dug in, with two of their platoons just outside Caira village.

This development led the Americans to shift their effort north to support the troops around Caira, the attack to be led by 756th Tank Battalion. On the morning of 29 January Company A, under the command of Captain French G. Lewis, set off along a log corduroy road laid previously by their engineers, Staff Sergeant James L. Harris' 3rd Platoon in the lead. Around 7.30am, with his other tanks following at 15-yard intervals, Harris' tank entered a section of the road that had become flooded where it crossed the Rapido and successfully negotiated this obstacle. He then swung left towards the barracks, the next three tanks of his platoon conforming to his movements. After him, Lewis' tank crossed successfully, as did Sergeant Mack N. Corbitt, though his tank was to be the last over. When Sergeant Oscar Hood's tank reached the middle of the ford the road gave way beneath his tank, causing his tank to slide to the right where it ended up blocking the ford.

This was not the end of their troubles however. Just as Corbitt's tank caught up with Lewis' tank, the latter was struck twice by armour-piercing rounds, killing the loader and wounding Lewis and the gunner. Then in short succession the tanks commanded by Staff Sergeant Thomas P. Ames, Sergeant Raymond V. Galbraith and Sergeant Howard A. Harrison were hit and knocked out, the latter going up in flames. This would have continued were it not for Corbitt who spotted an assault gun by the corner of walled cemetery and knocked it out.

This left the Americans in a difficult situation. Another company from 168th Infantry Regiment had also crossed the river but now had no real tank support. It was then that someone came up with the idea of using the dry Rapido River channel. Their engineers blew a gap in the riverbed beside the bridge the Germans had demolished earlier and destroyed a small concrete footbridge further downstream. This completed, late in the afternoon seventeen tanks from Company C, 756th Tank Battalion and a further nine from Company C, 760th Tank Battalion entered the dry riverbed, drove down it and then burst out onto the open ground, all guns blazing. This not only took the Germans by surprise but the dug-in American infantry as well and it took a few minutes for the Americans to realize what was happening. But within minutes they were out of their foxholes and off in pursuit of the tanks, moving forward in their track marks. By evening the Americans had cleared up the area around the cemetery and, with reinforcements, they succeeded in gaining footholds on the lower slopes of Points 156 and 213. These they took the following day.

It was at this point that the American attack split in two. On 1 February 168th Infantry Regiment, with support from 760th Tank Battalion, cleared out the village of

Caira. From there 168th Infantry began their assault on the Cassino massif itself, securing the summit of Monte Castelone two days later. Simultaneously with this 133th Infantry Regiment and 756th Tank Battalion struck southwards towards the Cassino township clearing out the German defensive positions along the road as they proceeded but the barracks proved to be another matter. Here they ran up against German infantry supported by three StuG IIIs from Oberleutnant Edwin Metzger's 3 Zug of 2 Batterie, StuG-Abt 242. Metzger's guns held out till that night then pulled out, though not without some difficulty. One of his StuG IIIs had thrown a track, so he stationed his other two assault guns facing the road while the crew of the other set to with sledgehammers, replaced the track and then departed.

Nevertheless some Germany infantry remained in the barracks and were not driven out till the next day. This achieved, with some tanks from Company B, 756th Tank Battalion on the road and Company C tanks in the riverbed, they and 168th Infantry set off for the town but were forced to return to the quarry after discovering that the road beyond it had been partially blown out. Company C fared no better as they found their progress blocked by the remains of a small concrete bridge. They withdrew after the turret hatch of one of the tanks was struck by a round from Gefreiter Teppe's assault gun.

That night Sweeting ordered the tanks in again, eight from Company A setting out after dark with thirty-eight infantry in support. The Germans let four tanks enter the town before knocking out the fifth with an anti-tank gun, leading those in the town to believe they were trapped. Fire from another anti-tank gun forced the infantry and the remaining tanks to pull back to the quarry. Shortly afterwards Metzger and some of his men located three of the tanks in a small square but when their attempt to knock one out with a Panzerschreck failed they set off towards the square armed with a MG42 machine gun, grenades and signal flares. Once there they fired at the tank cupolas, set off the flares and tossed grenades onto the tanks, forcing their crews to surrender. At this point the fourth Sherman swung around and headed back towards the square but ran into a ditch. With signs of it overturning its crew abandoned it and escaped. Leaving this tank, as it proved unrecoverable, Metzger's men drove the other three tanks back to their positions around the Jail (this building has generally been referred to as the Jail, although whether it was actually one or not is not clear)

On the morning of 3 February a company from 133th Infantry Regiment entered the town only to be driven out again by German tanks. That afternoon the Americans tried again but. Major Welborn Dolvin's tank emerged round the corner from the quarry it was struck by a round in the transmission, killing the driver and setting it on fire. The next four managed to slip past it and with infantry in support reached the outskirts of Cassino. There the infantry, now reduced to no more than a dozen men, cleared and then occupied the first four or five houses. Permission was sought to withdraw but this was denied, so they held their position for the rest of the night. However, when no reinforcements arrived the next morning they withdrew to a small streambed, only to re-enter the town later that afternoon.

Over the next few days the Americans worked their way further into the town, clearing it block by block, till on 7 February an attempt was made to launch a combined tank/infantry assault on the Jail and a building known as the town hall. The Germans, however, spotted the tanks just as they started to move forward and ordered two of their StuG IIIs forward. Within minutes one was seen moving across a square in the middle of the town. Shortly afterwards a second one appeared along the main street, stopping just behind a slight rise. This created a problem for the Shermans as their shells either ricocheted off the road in front or sailed right over the top of it. Just as the Shermans were bringing their guns to bear on it the StuG III opened fire and within a matter of seconds three of the tanks had been knocked out. Colonel Sweeting on the hill above tried to get an anti-tank gun onto the assault gun but his artillery liaison man could not make contact with the anti-tank gun. Then as they watched the StuG III backed behind a building, turned around and drove off.

While the Americans had been working to secure a foothold in the town, they were also trying to secure Castle Hill, first establishing themselves on Point 175 on 5 February. On 8 February the Japanese-Americans, having taken over from 1st Battalion, attacked Castle Hill, eventually taking control of Point 165 under the cover of smoke. Things soon changed for the worse when the wind shifted, clearing the smoke, bringing them under intense fire from the monastery. To add to their woes a StuG III broke cover from some buildings and opened fire on them. At that point Private Masao Awakuni crept forward and knocked it out with a bazooka. Nevertheless the intense fire from above did not abate. In the end they were forced to hold on until nightfall when they were able to withdraw.

Over the next few days the Americans managed to push a further 200 yards into the town. On 11 February the eight or nine Shermans of 756th Tank Battalion began blasting the Jail with an experimental HE round fitted with a delayed-action fuse; the same round they had used to blow away the outside wall of the castle. The next day the infantry went in and captured the Jail and two other buildings near it.

A day or two later the Americans attempted to extend their hold on the Cassino further and as a preliminary to this ordered Sergeant Haskell O. Oliver to blow a few holes in some buildings just beyond the Jail. Haskell set off in his Sherman but just as they moved out to cross a road an AP round flashed past. Sweeting, having seen that it had come from a PzKpfw IV, ordered him to take on the tank. Haskell and crew got out to locate the tank themselves, then climbed back in the tank where the loader pulled out AP rounds from their racks and laid them out ready.

The driver then thrust down hard on the throttle, drove the tank out at full speed and aligned it rapidly on the German tank, before bringing his own one to stop with a lurch. After the tank ceased rocking backwards and forward the gunner started slamming shell after shell at the tank, the first one being fired off as the sights were still moving across the target, and within minutes the PzKpfw IV had been eliminated. Later that night, their mission successfully completed, Oliver learned that one of the Germans captured in the subsequent fighting had asked to see the tank with the new automatic-fire gun!

By now, however, the American attack in the town had run its course. The Germans had reached the point of exhaustion too. On the Cassino massif, where the battle had been seesawing for days, the Americans had finally lost the strategically Point 593 along Snakeshead Ridge after taking it on 5 February. Now they were to be progressively replaced in the town by Lieutenant General Sir Bernard Freyberg's 2nd New Zealand Division and on the Cassino massif by Major General Francis Tuker's 4th Indian Division, both of which had been brought over from the Adriatic.

The castle on Rocca Ianula, here under fire prior to the US attack on the town, was a prime observation point for the Germans. (NARA)

Among the tanks lost during the attack over the Rapido River on 27 January was this M4 Sherman from Company B, 756th Tank Battalion, which got stuck in a ditch beside the road. (NARA; PISM)

Another victim of the attempt to cross the Rapido River during the attack on 27 January was this M4 Sherman from 756th Tank Battalion. (NARA)

After his ammunition ran out during the 27 January attack over the Rapido River, Lieutenant Wayne B. Henry's tank slipped off this bridge and was then knocked out by anti-tank fire from the barracks. (NARA)

This Sturmgeschütz III from Sturmgeschütz-Abteilung 242 beside the Caira–Cassino road north of the Barracks is possibly the one that knocked out several tanks from 756th Tank Battalion during the attack over the Rapido river on 29 January. (PISM)

Prior to the attack on the town on 3 February Shermans from 756th and 760th Tank Battalions gathered in a stone quarry north of Cassino.

With the attack in progress the column of Shermans from 756th and 760th Tank Battalions move out along the Cassino–Caira road from the quarry.

Problems entering the town forced the tanks to halt along the road, while the collapse of a bridge in the dried up bed of the Rapido River blocked the tanks using that line of approach.

After the fall of Cassino on 18 May these M4A1 Shermans were found around the northern end of the town. (PISM; NAMNZ)

Two of the M4 Shermans lost by the Americans were subsequently pushed off the road. (PISM)

One of the M4A1 Shermans from the US 756th Tank Battalion, knocked out near the Jail was overturned in the subsequent bombing of the town. (ATL)

StuG-Abt 242 stationed one of its StuG IIIs on Rocca Ianula, mainly for observational purposes. It was knocked out by a bazooka by Private Masao Awakuni from 100th Nisei Battalion on 8 February 1944. It appears to have suffered further in the subsequent bombardments, as the follwing five images show. (NARA; PISM; G Kingscote)

The Germans also stationed a number of tanks in Cassino as the remains of a PzKpfw IV below Castle Hill testify. (PISM)

Chapter Four

The Second Battle

The arrival of the New Zealanders and Indians at Cassino spelled a new phase in the battle for Cassino. On 19 January, they had been combined into a new formation, the New Zealand Corps under the command of Freyberg. It also included Combat Command B of US 1st Armored Division, comprising 8th Armored Infantry Regiment, 753rd and 760th Tank Battalions and 701st Tank Destroyer Battalion. The New Zealanders, now commanded by Brigadier Howard Kippenberger, started to move into positions around Monte Trocchio on 3 February. Two weeks after this the British 78th Division arrived and were incorporated into the new corps.

With a German counter-offensive expected within days at Anzio-Nettuno, there was pressure on Freyberg to continue the offensive at Cassino to prevent the Germans drawing troops away from the Gustav Line. Freyberg eventually decided to renew the attack on Points 593 and 569 with 5th Indian Division, now under the command of Brigadier Harry Dimoline, and then secure the monastery. From there they were to drive downhill, cut Route 6 and then link up with 2nd NZ Division advancing from the vicinity of the railway station. This was to be secured by 28th (Maori) Battalion and once the demolitions along the railway embankment had been repaired 19th NZ Armoured Regiment was to assist in the expansion of the bridgehead to include the southern part of Cassino up to Route 6. After this Combat Command B was to begin the breakout phase into the Liri Valley.

A key part of this plan, and the most controversial part, was Freyberg's insistence that the monastery be bombed. Though the Germans had not occupied it, they had built their defences very close to it and were storing ammunition in caves below the building itself. Not that this was at all obvious to the Allies. There was a strong belief in the Allied camp that the Germans were using the building, even if it was just as an observation point. Whatever the case, the sight of the imposing building overlooking them was somehow symbolic and the thought was that its destruction would ease the minds of those trying to secure it. There was also the view in some quarters that the Germans would eventually be forced to incorporate it into their defences. Clark, however, was against the bombing of the monastery and had made that plain to Freyberg. Nevertheless, Tuker, the former commander of 4th Indian

Division, pleaded with Freyberg to bomb the monastery. This prompted Freyberg to contact Clark about arranging air support for the operation but instead reached Clark's Chief-of-Staff Major General Alfred M. Gruenther. Gruenther was not happy when he learned it was to be the monastery and tried unsuccessfully to contact Clark at Anzio. In the meantime Freyberg contacted General Sir Harold Alexander's 15th Army Group headquarters. Alexander was supportive of the bombing if Freyberg considered it a military necessity and, though Clark did object to the bombing when he eventually found out, Alexander overrode him.

Originally set to begin on the night of 13/14 February, the attack had to be delayed twice. On the first occasion this was because of a strong attack by the Germans against the Americans on Monte Castellone. This in turn put back the relief of the Americans on Snakeshead ridge by 7th Indian Brigade until the night of the 13/14th because they were needed to back up the Americans on Castellone. Then a major storm in the area caused a further postponement. The bombing was reset to take place on the morning of the 15th, even though this was not to the Indian Division's satisfaction. They had expected the monastery to be bombed on the afternoon of the following day and had planned to withdraw their troops on the night of 15/16 February but now there was no time to change that.

In the end the bombing took place as scheduled on 15 February, the first wave of 142 B-17 Flying Fortresses arriving at 9.25am and continuing their attack for half an hour. After this there was a brief respite of half an hour before the second wave of forty B-26 Marauders and forty-seven B-25 Mitchells arrived and continued to bomb the monastery until 1.32pm. By the time they were finished the monastery was in ruins. Of the German defenders outside the walls, most were killed, along with 300 or so of the 1,000 refugees and monks inside the building. One company of infantry from 7th Indian Brigade 300 yards away also suffered twenty-four casualties.

Though the monastery was the prime objective, the Indians were committed to securing Points 593 and 569 first. As an attack in daylight would have been suicidal, their first attempt was not made until that evening. On that occasion 1st Battalion Royal Sussex Regiment soon came under intense fire from the troops from General Richard Heidrich's 1 Fallschirmjäger-Division on the summit. After running out of grenades were forced back to their original positions.

The following night their attack was delayed until 11pm to allow one of their mule trains to come forward with more grenades. Then as they were forming up some Allied artillery shells failed to clear Snakeshead Ridge and landed amongst them. Once again they came under intense fire from the summit of Point 593 but this time managed to break into the main defensive position. However, they were soon forced out after hand-to-hand fighting.

The final attempt on Point 593 and the monastery was made on the night of 17/18 February, on a wider front with two battalions from 5th Indian Brigade under their command. Despite the deployment of additional troops they failed to make a dent in the German lines. While 4th Battalion 6th Rajputana Rifles were beaten back in their attack on Point 593, troops from 1st Battalion 2nd Gurkha Rifles ran into a booby-trapped minefield in their attempt on the monastery. They suffered heavily before withdrawing. By morning the attack had run its course with 7th Indian Brigade having gained nothing for their effort.

This attack that night was launched in conjunction with 2nd NZ Division's attack on the railway station. At 8.45pm A and B Companies from 28th (Maori) Battalion set off along the railway embankment. B Company made good progress, despite the creeks, drains, swamps and a minefield, and an hour later reached the station yards. After a short sharp fight they secured the Round House (the engine shed) and station buildings, driving out Panzergrenadier-Regiment III/361. Beyond there, however, they were unable to make any headway. A Company, over to their left, attacked but failed to take the Hummocks to the south of the Round House.

The Germans responded by sending around some assault engineers from 71 Infanterie-Division. Accompanying them were two StuG IIIs but these had to drop out with track damage, leaving the engineers to carry on alone. Around 4.00am the assault engineers met up with some infantry from Panzergrenadier-Regiment 361, and together crossed the Gari River by way of the wrecked railway bridge. The combined force then launched their attack on the Round House but were beaten back under intense fire from the Maori troops inside, losing several men. Renewed attempts also failed, at which point the Germans were forced to retreat.

While things had gone relatively well for the Maori in the station yards, a serious situation was developing further back with the preparation of the railway embankment for tanks. The engineers had initially been forced to withdraw to allow the Americans to put down a short artillery barrage and then to let the Maori troops to assemble prior to their advance. Thus it was not until 11.15pm that they were able to launch their first bridge over a small canal, only to have it damaged twice by dozers. This took two hours fix and another hour elapsed before they were able to get bridging material to the Rapido itself. By 5.30am the bridge was ready, as were the next three breaches along the embankment. Half an hour later, with the last two breaches still to be repaired, the Maori companies requested permission to withdraw but this was denied, the engineers being withdrawn instead.

Shortly after dawn the Germans launched a counter-attack from Cassino with three platoons of infantry covered by fire from two of the captured Shermans, the latter still in their US markings. This was broken up by an artillery concentration, just as the German infantry were forming up, and the tanks were driven off by medium artillery fire directed from a spotter plane.

This left the Maori troops in the railway station in a difficult position. The New Zealand artillery provided them with what support they could, covering the area in a smoke screen. Unfortunately the Germans were also able to use it to move more troops into the area. Around 3.15pm they launched a second attack across the Gari along the railway embankment, while two StuG IIIs from StuG-Abt 242 came in from the town. Within a short space of time they had forced their way into the station yards and overran the forward sections of Maori infantry. Faced with this onslaught the surviving Maori troops abandoned their positions and pulled back along the railway line. Thus ended the second battle for Cassino.

The opening of the Second Battle of Monte Cassino on 15 February was heralded by the bombing of the monastery. (Stratton Morrin)

StuG-Abt 242 soon put their captured Shermans to good use but for a time kept them in their original markings. (Wolfgang Loof)

Two of the Shermans were used by StuG-Abt 242 in their counter-attack against 28th Maori Battalion at the railway station on 18 February. (Wolfgang Loof)

The turret was eventually removed from one of the Shermans so it could be used as a munitions carrier. (Wolfgang Loof)

One of the Shermans captured by StuG-Abt 242 was moved to the south of Cassino and attached to their Sturmhaubitz platoon. (Karlheinz Muench)

Chapter Five

The Third Battle

For the next attempt on Cassino by the New Zealand Corps Freyberg decided to concentrate his effort on securing a passage into the Liri Valley by pushing through the town. Initially the monastery was only to be a secondary objective to be secured if an opportunity arose, something that upset Clark. As a result Freyberg was forced revise his plan by switching the focus of the attack of 4th Indian Division, now under the command of Major General Alexander Galloway. Instead of working side by side with the New Zealanders they were now to launch a direct assault on the monastery by way of Castle Hill and Hangman's Hill (the stanchion for the monastery cablecar). A late addition was an armoured thrust through a valley behind Snakeshead Ridge, codenamed Operation Revenge, to be launched once the monastery had been secured and there were signs of the front collapsing. The assault on the town was entrusted to 6th NZ Brigade, advancing under a lifting barrage to a line running from the railway station to the Baron's Palace on Route 6 to the south of the town. Once this line had been reached Combat Command B of US 1st Armored Division was to pass through and swing out into the Liri Valley. Then 20th NZ Armoured Regiment and 22nd NZ Motor Battalion were to drive south to Sant'Angelo and link up with 78th Division. In what was to be another controversial move this was to be preceded by the bombing of Cassino township. Freyberg was adamant that this was an essential part of the process to clear the town, which was held by II/3 Fallschirmjäger-Regiment, but there were concerns that it would make it difficult for his armour to operate in the town. Freyberg's response was that it would also make it difficult for German armour too.

Thus, around 8.30am on the morning of 15 March the troops in the valley were woken once more by the drone of approaching aircraft as the bombers made their final approach to Cassino. For the next three and a half hours the planes dropped 992 tons of high explosive on the town, after which the artillery took over and added to the destruction. By the end of this Cassino had been reduced to ruins. Their armour in Cassino suffered too. Sturmgeschütze-Brigade 242 had three assault guns from 2 Zug, 3 Batterie in the town, though only that of Wachmeister Schumann's in the garage of the Palazzo Iucci, by the Hotel Continental/Excelsior, surviving the bombing unscathed. Wachtmeister Reiter's StuG III ended up trapped inside a building in the complex of the Chiesa di San Antonio, while he and his crew disappeared and were never seen again. Wachmiester Teppe was badly wounded and had to be evacuated, while his driver disappeared in the bombing. His StuG III in the Sopportico Capocci, opposite the Nunnery, was damaged and could not be repaired so its ammunition was transferred to Schumann's vehicle.

Things did not go well for New Zealand armour either. Their supporting infantry from 25th NZ Battalion had gone in behind a lifting artillery barrage following the cessation of the bombing. This enabled the infantry from A Company to return to their old positions in the Jail but when they tried to push further in they ran into trouble. Though the German paratroopers had suffered heavily in the bombing enough of them managed to struggle out of the ruins to face the assaulting troops. Nevertheless by mid-afternoon some New Zealand infantry had managed to reach the northern branch of Route 6.

The tanks from 5 and 6 Troops, 19th NZ Armoured Regiment that were to go in with A Company 25th NZ Battalion had less success. They were unable to get in along their designated route because the bombing had destroyed the ford over the Rapido. As a result they were forced to retrace their steps and make their way down the Cassino-Caira road, the approach route taken by 7 and 8 Troops. Of the latter, 7 Troop had managed to work their way forward to a position halfway between the Jail and Route 6. Beyond that, though, the craters and debris from wrecked buildings blocked further progress. A Valentine bridgelayer was called up but the craters were so large it could not span them. Instead the crews were forced to get out of their tanks and, under the cover of smoke, clear a route with picks and shovels to where they could provide fire support for the infantry.

In a similar manner to 7 Troop the tanks of 8 Troop were able to work their way forward to the Post Office. There they met up with infantry from B Company, 25th NZ Battalion. They had come under fire from Castle Hill that forced them to take up positions in a school just short of the Nunnery. The tanks provided fire support for a platoon from B Company in their attack on the Nunnery, to no avail as the platoon was eventually forced out by its German occupants.

More success was had by D Company, who, in the absence of support by 7 Troop, launched an attack on Castle Hill. Working their way up, simultaneously from two sides, they took it after a short sharp fight. That night 1st Battalion 4th Essex Regiment from 5th Indian Brigade replaced the New Zealanders in the castle. Later 1st Battalion/9th Gurkha Rifles passed through these positions and advanced further up, eventually reaching Hangman's Hill, where they immediately began digging in. That night, too, 26th NZ Battalion moved into the town and took up positions in the Post Office and municipal buildings north of the Piazza Principe Amedeo (the Botanical Gardens).

A company from 24th NZ Battalion also entered the town on the first day of the attack and the following day, after linking up with 25th NZ Battalion under Castle Hill, pushed another 150–200m closer to the Hotel Continental. Over to their left the Germans tried to retake the Municipal Buildings but were driven off, losing several dead in the process. Later some Germans managed to enter and occupy the Chiesa del Carmine (the Convent) where they proceeded to snipe at the New Zealanders, though not for too long. Around noon 1 Troop, A Squadron, 19th NZ Armoured Regiment, under Lieutenant Stratton Morrin, crossed the Rapido over a newly erected Bailey Bridge on Route 6 only to be held up by a crater further along the road until this bridged by a Valentine bridgelayer. Morrin crossed over first in his tank but tilted the bridge in the process, preventing his other tanks from using it. Beyond that his progress was blocked by another crater just short of the Convent forcing him make his way forward on foot. He was only just prevented from entering the Convent by 14th Platoon of 26th NZ Battalion who were about to launch their assault on it. Morrin hastily retraced his steps, shelled the building, his tanks killing four Germans and driving the rest off. The Convent was then occupied by 26th NZ Battalion.

On 17 March the stage was set for the most spectacular part of the whole of the battle for the town. The day began with 24th and 25th NZ Battalions pushing off through the early morning mist towards the Botanical Gardens. For support they had 10 Troop, 19th NZ Armoured Regiment. One of the tanks threw a track on entering the Botanical Gardens and the other became inextricably struck in some soft going. Still, with their fire support, they were able to assist in the clearance of buildings around the Gardens. Within an hour the infantry had managed to cross a branch of the Gari River but beyond there became pinned by strong fire from the buildings around the Hotel Continental.

With the gardens now clear 26th NZ Battalion was free to launch its attack on the railway station, though it proved a bit of a struggle to just cross to the Convent because of the intense fire coming down Route 6 from the Hotel Continental area. Instead the lead companies became disorganized as they raced over the road and needed time to sort themselves out. Fortunately A Squadron, 19th NZ Armoured Regiment under Major Jack Thodey had managed to move some more tanks in the town. So the attack was led off at 11.00am. by Lieutenant Jim Furness' 4 Troop, though at first he had to crawl through the rubble just to find the track leading to the Viale Dante, the main road to the railway station. Thereafter he led his tank on foot until he discovered some mines at the junction of it with the Viale Dante, which he and Corporal Bill Forbes cleared by hand, unbeknown to them under the watchful gaze of a German anti-tank gun crew in the Hotel des Roses. Not that there was much that Gefreiter Günther Rabiger or the other gun crew could do about it as their commander had locked the traverse of the gun while he gone off to the toilet. Furness and his other tank then drove on to the railway station unscathed, where they proceeded to shoot up the Germans in the Round House and on the Hummocks.

With no sign of 26th Battalion Furness was in need of support, so 2 Troop, under Lieutenant 'Dib' Beswick, was dispatched but by now the commander of Rabiger's gun had returned and his anti-tank gun was ready. First to be hit was Beswick's tank, which was struck twice by armour-piercing rounds before catching fire. Shortly afterwards Corporal Garth Ryder's tank was hit and set on fire. Both crews evacuated their tanks successfully after which Ryder found a submachine gun on a dead German and, with Beswick, stalked and overcame an enemy post capturing its seven occupants.

Thodey then sent 3 Troop forward. Sergeant Frank Milne's tank made it safely to the railway station Lieutenant Ron Griggs' tank was hit a large piece of shrapnel jamming the suspension, so he changed tanks with Milne and drove forward until blocked by the floodwaters of the Gari River. About this point in the battle Schumann's StuG III emerged from its lair and opened up on Ryder's tank causing it to burst into flames. Schumann then turned his attention to the next tank to appear, that of Corporal Gordon Hubbard, hitting it as it attempted to pass Beswick's Sherman, causing it to collide with the tank. Hubbard's tank then slipped off the road and fell sideways into a large water-filled crater. Of the crew only two survived. The driver got out and took shelter in a water-filled crater leaving the wireless operator, Trooper Michael Cooney, trapped inside the turret; that night it took five hours to cut him out.

For a time the tanks held the station area alone but over the next few hours small groups of infantry from 26th NZ Battalion made their way across the open ground to them. One platoon of infantry then raced over and cleaned out the Round House but was blocked from any further movement by heavy fire from the east and west; that is until 4 Troop came to their aid and silenced the fire. At that point a second platoon dashed over to the Hummocks and overcame resistance on it.

By 18 March, however, it was apparent that the attack was beginning to stall. With their supply route in danger of being cut off, the Gurkhas on Hangman's Hill were in a perilous position and Galloway was not willing to commit them to their attack on the Monastery until the supply line was secure. This depended on the town being cleared but at this stage Freyberg was reluctant to commit 5th NZ Brigade as this was required for the exploitation phase. Instead most of the day was spent by 25th NZ Battalion rooting out Germans below Castle Hill, aided by some tanks from 19th NZ Armoured Regiment. Above the town a company from 24th NZ Battalion launched a daylight attack on the Hotel Continental in an attempt to clear out its defenders but they soon came under intense fire. This forced one platoon to pull back up the hill and pinned down another. Efforts to break the deadlock with tank fire failed and the New Zealand infantry went to ground until nightfall when they were able to get away. The Germans attempted to retake the railway station, sending in sixty-three men but half of them were killed or wounded by their own mortars while just moving up. The survivors were beaten back with heavy losses by 26th NZ Battalion

Later that afternoon of the 18th Freyberg finally relented and committed 28th (Maori) Battalion, from 5th NZ Brigade, the battalion moving into town that evening. Galloway also agreed to renewing the attack on the Monastery but this was to take place only after 1st Battalion 6th Rajputana Rifles had relieved 1st Battalion 4th Essex on Castle Hill and the latter had moved up to Hangman's Hill. This changeover was successfully completed the following morning but the Essex troops had just started to make their way up to the Gurkhas when they spotted a large force of German paratroopers sweeping down towards the Castle. Most of the Essex troops continued upwards but those that returned to Castle Hill became embroiled in a struggle that lasted for most of that day. Under these circumstances there was no way that the attack on the monastery could go ahead so Freyberg called it off. The tank attack, however, did go ahead and, though it did meet with some success at first, also came to naught (see Chapter 6).

Very little progress was made in the town that day either. The Maori Battalion struck down Route 6 the direction of the Hotel Continental and though they made some progress failed to take the area around the hotel. It was during this engagement that their supporting tanks from 19th NZ Armoured Regiment claimed the destruction of two German tanks, one of them near the Hotel Continental. With the aid of Stratton Morrin's tank they did secure the surrender of eighty-odd paratroopers holed up in a building with a partially-buried assault gun. By now Freyberg had come to the realisation that he would have to commit the rest of 5th NZ Brigade so arrangements were made for 11th Brigade of 78th Division to take over the New Zealand sector south of Cassino.

Over the next few days further attempts were made to clear the area around the Hotel Continental and the tangle of buildings under Castle Hill, though with ever-decreasing success. A joint attack by 21st and 24th NZ Battalions on 20 March towards the former was soon brought to a halt under a hail of fire. The Maori Battalion did manage to stop an encircling movement by some Germans with the help of their supporting armour. In an attempt to clear the last pocket below the Castle 23rd and 25th NZ Battalions managed to get to within 100m of the base of Castle Hill but could get no further. The following day 21st NZ Battalion launched another attempt on the Hotel Continental position. One of their platoons became pinned down in a shell hole by fire at which point Schumann's StuG III drove out of its lair and opened fire on the rest of the battalion further back. With them safely neutralized, the Germans rushed out to the shell hole and forced the platoon to surrender.

Later the battalion did have one success. They discovered an assault gun in a school building within the San Antonio complex when its occupants started up its engines to charge its batteries; the Germans had apparently been using it as a radio link. Lieutenant Jock McPhail's tank was called up and brewed up the assault gun with a few rounds. After this McPhail's tank became hung up on the edge of a crater outside the school where it was in danger of slipping into it. McPhail and crew were forced to remain in the tank until they could carefully evacuate it under the cover of dark.

Over the next few days the struggle for the town began to wind down. By 23 March, with little further progress having been made, the attack was called off and the troops went over to the defensive.

Though the town was often shrouded in smoke, from time to time parts of it would appear, in this view the Hotel des Roses can be seen on the left and to the right the castle on Rocca Ianula. (ATL)

On the morning of 15 March 1944 the Allies launched their strategic bomber force on the town of Cassino. (ATL)

Wachtmeister Reiter's StuG III from Sturmgeschütze-Brigade 242 was entombed in the rubble of the Chiesa di San Antonio complex by the bombing. (IWM)

Paratroopers inspect Wachtmeister Teppe's StuG III in the Sopportico Capocci, opposite the Chiesa di Santa Scholastica (the Nunnery) after the bombing of the town. (Marco Marzilli)

Damage to Cassino as a result of the bombing blocked the entry of C Squadron, 19 NZ Armoured Regiment, on the Cassino-Caira road, into the town. (ATL)

During the initial move into Cassino this Sherman III from B Squadron was abandoned on Parallel Road just after it crossed the Rapido River. (George Andrews)

During the morning of 17 March Lieutenant Peter Brown's tank from 10 Troop, C Squadron, 19th NZ Armoured Regiment threw a track on the Via Arigni while taking part in an attack on the Botanical Gardens. (Frank J. Davis)

While Lieutenant Jim Furness and his sergeant made it safely to the railway station on 17 March, those of Lieutenant 'Dib' Beswick (foreground) and Corporal Garth Ryder were knocked on the Viale Dante. (Rod Eastgate)

'Dib' Beswick's tank on the road into the railway station. The building behind is the remains of the terminus of the aerial cableway for the monastery. (Rod Eastgate)

Lieutenant Dib Beswick's tank from 2 Troop, A Squadron, 19th Armoured Regiment on the Viale Dante. (PISM)

Corporal Garth Ryder's tank on the Vaile Dante shows evidence of having caught fire. (PISM)

After the capture of the railway station Jim Furness took this photo of the Round House (the railway engine house) from the turret of his tank. (Jim Furness)

Lieutenant Jim Furness (standing on the left) with his crew after getting out of Cassino for the first time. From left to right, on the turret: Stan Furley and Lindsay Miles; in front of the tank: Furness, Bill Forbes and Leo Strong. (Jim Furness)

During the fighting in the town this PzKpfw IV from Panzer-Abteilung 115, 15. Panzergrenadier-Regiment broke its right-hand track while responding to a New Zealand attack on their positions around the Hotel Continental.

The Germans soon covered it with smoke, allowing the crew to repair its track under fire.

After an unsuccessful attempt to recover its scissors bridge on Route 6 on the night of 18/19 March, this Valentine bridgelayer tank missed the road and slipped into this crater. (George Andrews)

Another New Zealand Valentine bridgelayer tank capsized in this crater during the fighting in Cassino. (George Andrews)

These three photos of Schumann's StuG III was taken on one of the occasions that it emerged from the Palazzo Iucci (beside the Hotel Excelsior/Continental) to engage New Zealand forces. (George Schmitz)

Lieutenant Jock McPhail's Sherman III ended up in this crater beside the Chiesa di San Antonio after knocking out a StuG III in the Scholastica di San Antonio. (George Andrews)

When Lieutenant Jim Furness and his crew went into Cassino for a second time, their tank capsized in a crater, flipping onto its turret in the process. It was eventually buried during the subsequent restoration of the town. (George Andrews)

Chapter Six

The Cavendish Road Attack

The problems with supply to the troops on Snakeshead Ridge during the Second Battle drove 5th Indian Division to upgrade two peasant footpaths that had been used by their porters and mule trains. Both led off from a rough track through a gully near the Barracks to the village of Caira. One of them, dubbed 'Rorkee Road', that ran directly up to Cole Maiola was upgraded to take Jeeps. The second ran up from the village of Caira through the Valle Pozzo Alvito. Part way up it split into two, an upper track that crossed a sheer, 60-foot long rock face of a dry watercourse and a lower track that rejoined the main track via a steep gradient. On 17 March 4th Indian Field Company set about widening the lower track to take mules, while developing the upper track to take Jeeps. The upper track was eventually named 'Cavendish Road' by the Indian Commander Royal Engineers, Lieutenant-Colonel E.E, Stenhouse, after the name of the road in which his father lived in Bournemouth.

Concern about their ability to deal with the rock face around the dry watercourse led the Indians to contact Colonel Frederick Hanson, Commander New Zealand Engineers. After inspecting the site Hanson came up with the idea of enlarging the upper road so that it could be used to get tanks, including Shermans, above and behind the monastery. He sent the Indians 2nd Platoon, 6th NZ Field Company who set about blasting a way through the rock face of the watercourse with explosives. The work was finally complete on 11 March and with it Operation Revenge was drawn up. This task was assigned to 7th Indian Brigade Reconnaissance Squadron, under Major Malcolm Cruikshank, and Company D, 760th US Tank Battalion, under Lieutenant Herman R. Crowder. While purely a tank force, there was provision for reinforcing it with a company of infantry from 1st Sussex Regiment.

Thus it was on the night of 15/16 March that both armoured units made their way up Cavendish Road to their laying-up areas. The Indian squadron settled into Madras Circus, a bowl nestled between Monte Castellone and Colle Maoila, while the American tanks parked up along the road between the dried up watercourse and the final bend into Madras Circus. Their support platoon of M7 Priest 105mm self-propelled guns under Lieutenant Victor F. Hipkiss had to remain in the village of

Caira. With the failure of the Gurkhas to advance beyond Hangman's Hill Operation Revenge had to be postponed. Instead their tanks were covered with camouflage nets by some Indian engineers who had accompanied them.

As late as midday on 18 March the situation was unchanged. Revenge Force was informed that with the monastery still in German hands no attack seemed likely. Shortly after receiving this message, however, a lone German aircraft spotted Crowder's line of tanks, flew down and strafed them. Then at 2.00pm they were informed that the attack was on for the next day, and a new commander had been assigned to them, Colonel John Adye (the acting Colonel Royal Artillery of the Indian Division) and that C Squadron of 20th NZ Armoured Regiment, under Major Pat Barton, was to join the force. To accommodate Adye's need for direct communication back to 4th Indian Division an extra radio was installed in Sergeant Owen Hughes' tank from 9 Troop, C Squadron, Hughes being forced to command it from the spare driver's position.

In the early hours of 19 March the tanks of the column threw off their camouflage nets and resumed their march up Cavendish Road. In the lead were the three Shermans and five Stuarts of the Indian recce squadron, while Hipkiss' Priests followed up in the rear. For additional support they had a D-7 tractor and two D-6 bulldozers. These soon proved their worth when Sergeant Carrigan's Sherman from the Indian squadron started having problems with a slipping clutch. After holding the column up for half an hour one the D-6s towed it up to the top. Further back the last New Zealand tank, Corporal Rex Miller's Sherman from 9 Troop, C Squadron, slipped off the road just after they set off and had to be left behind.

Once all had reached Madras Circus the column came to a halt to await the outcome of the attack on the monastery but not for long. When it appeared to be failing Freyberg ordered Operation Revenge to go ahead. At that point Crowder's tanks led off from Madras Circus through a small gap (the first 'Bottleneck') where a narrow spur ran down from Phantom Ridge. Once through the gap 3rd Platoon, under Lieutenant John A. Crews, swung to the left towards Phantom House, the remains of a building that was being used as an observation post, but soon ran into trouble. In the steeply terraced terrain one Stuart threw a track and when Crew's platoon moved forward again another came off its tracks, followed by Crew's tank. At that point Lieutenant de Right's 2nd Platoon and Hipkiss' M7 Priests moved up and opened fired on the house, bringing it down in short order. Lieutenant Chester M. Wright then went forward to determine if a way could be found up to Phantom House and thence onwards to Villa San Lucia. When that proved fruitless they all returned to the main force in the valley.

While the Americans were thus engaged with Phantom House, Barton's C Squadron set off in the direction of Massa Albaneta. Led by Second Lieutenant Jack

Hazlett's 11 Troop, they proceeded up the valley setting off the carefully laid S-mines, which went off under their tracks like firecrackers. Some 300 yards out of Madras Circus, Hazlett's tank slipped sideways off the road into a small ditch so he switched to his sergeant's tank. Hughes' tank with Adye on board threw one of its tracks, forcing Adye to transfer to one of the Indian tanks. Sergeant-Major Jock Laidlaw's Sherman also threw a track. Lieutenant Bill de Lautour then tried to climb a rock spur on Phantom Ridge to provide covering fire but his tank shed a track. He switched to his sergeant's tank. One of the Indian Shermans bellied in a bomb crater as well.

While the loss of some tanks early on was not too critical for the mission, the ditching of Hughes' tank was more serious as it meant that Adye had lost communication back to the division. In the end the Indians decided to fall back on the radio net, controlling both the Recce Squadron and C Squadron through Barton's second-in-command tank, with it acting as rear link as well. Though no infantry had been released at this stage the Indians had decided that things were looking favourable enough to release a company from 1st Battalion Royal Sussex to support the tank thrust. Setting up the link to them proved to be a problem, however. The Indians tried to string up a phone link with the Sussex company on Phantom Ridge but it was cut by a mortar bomb. The commander of the tank laying the line was also wounded so they abandoned this attempt. Crowder was also forced to switch to one of the turretless Indian Stuart tanks after the radio in his tank failed.

C Squadron then passed through the first 'Bottleneck', after which their column came under mortar fire, one round setting fire to the gear strapped to the back of Captain Jim Moodie's tank. Moodie, however, remained blissfully unaware of it until Crowder pulled alongside in the turretless Indian tank he was riding in and alerted him. Moodie armed himself with a fire extinguisher but when it had no effect, he kicked the burning gear off and climbed back into the turret.

Shortly after this the lead troop of C Squadron entered the second 'Bottleneck' in two-up formation, shooting up a machine-gun nest as they did so. Lieutenant Harold ('Buck') Renall and Corporal Dick Jones, leapfrogged forward in the lead, proceeding to swing their turrets left to pound the hillside. Very soon they found themselves on the saddle of the ridge overlooking Massa Albaneta, a steep gulley to the west ('Death Gulley') and the Liri Valley beyond. Here they halted and opened up on Massa Albaneta with their main guns while their spare drivers raked it with their .30 Brownings.

Once the rest of the squadron caught up, Barton ordered Renall's troop and Hazlett's two tanks down into the valley, the latter tasked with covering Massa Albaneta. With their ammunition running low, Renall and Jones proceeded down a narrow track, followed by Hazlett's and Corporal Reg Lennie's. Hazlett's tank was the first to get hit, a mortar round striking the engine compartment and setting its camouflage net on fire. Hazlett got out to extinguish it but he was cut down and killed by a burst of machine-gun fire. His crew then drove on till the tank was under the lee of Massa Abaneta. At that point it was struck by a Panzerschreck rocket and its crew bailed out, the driver and spare driver taking shelter under the tank, while the turret crew jumped into a shell hole and were never seen again. Lennie's tank fared slightly better. They had taken their tank over towards Massa Albaneta where a round from a Panzerschreck disabled one of their motors. They turned the tank around and attempted to get it out but their tank slipped sideways into a shell hole.

Shortly after that, their lack of ammunition proving critical and under heavy shelling, Renall's luck ran out. With his head partly out of the turret he was killed by a burst of machine-gun fire. The crew then turned around and headed back to the main body of the squadron, where they discovered that their radiator was leaking. As he was pulling out Jones' tank was hit by a round from a Panzerschreck. When Jones regained consciousness, his arm badly bleeding, he discovered his loader on the floor and the gunner slumped over the 75mm. Jones managed to swing the turret around so the driver could come through to the turret to apply a tourniquet to his arm and then went back and fired up both motors. Then they turned the tank around and headed back through the squadron and onto the forward casualty clearing station.

Now for a time there was a pause in activity as the headquarters of 4th Indian Division and NZ Corps began a debate on the whole operation. In fact by midday Barton's battered force of seven tanks had been in the saddle for some three hours. Barton contacted Adye, who ordered them back to Madras Circus but this was quickly countermanded by 7th Indian Brigade Headquarters. Apparently their division was still keen for the Gurkhas to push onto the monastery, possibly heartened by a report from a spotter plane had observed some tanks of Revenge Force on its way to the monastery. However, by 12.20pm it was apparent that the Indians were beginning to lose heart. Some doubt had started to infuse into the Indian's minds as to whether the tanks could actually make it around to the monastery particularly after the commander of 7th Indian Brigade said that he had exhausted every possibility of getting there.

In the meantime, with the higher command apparently paralysed by indecision, Barton focus was on rescuing the crews of his two tanks down by Massa Albaneta. One problem, though, was soon solved. Once the fire had gone out in Hazlett's tank, one of the crew climbed back through the hatch, tried the motors and got them going. The other crewman pointed out an enemy machine-gun team to Lennie, who took care of it. He then climbed back into the tank and they returned to the squadron on the saddle before heading back to Madras Circus. One of the other tanks tried to get down to Lennie's tank but the shelling was too heavy and, with signs of Germans with Panzerschecks, the attempt was abandoned. Then some tanks from the squadron put down smoke to cover the escape of Lennie and his crew but the heavy sniping put Lennie and his crew off the idea. Eventually, under covering fire, Wright from Company D and one of the Indian recce tanks raced down and rescued all of them.

Nothing happened until around 2.20pm when an intercept of a German radio transmission was received stating that eight tanks had broken through their main line of defence and that an infantry attack seemed probable. This seemed to galvanize the NZ Corps into action, though the plan was changed. Since the track round to the monastery considered to be too narrow for the Shermans, the decision was made to send the American Stuarts and if this failed to withdraw Revenge Force to Madras Circus before nightfall.

This was rather unfortunate as, through this period of Allied inactivity, the Germans had been busy. As soon as word of the tanks around Massa Albaneta had been received they had organized a party of pioneers and sent them up with more anti-tank weaponry. The commander of 14 Panzerjäger-Kompanie, Oberleutnant Raimund Eckel and Gefreiter Kammermann, was also sent to investigate.

Around 3.30pm Wright's 1st Platoon of Company D and the first section of 3rd Platoon under Crews started down the narrow down track towards Massa Albaneta. Coming around the first bend they shot up some Germans coming up the track towards them. Once on the flat they spread out. Crews' tank ended up well out in front, too far in front apparently, as he stopped the tank and ordered his driver to turn it round. As he was in the process of doing so Kammermann took aim with his panzerschreck. His first two rounds misfired but the third one went home, stopping Crews' tank in its tracks.

With no more rounds for the panzerschreck Eckel set off in search for something else to use against the tanks. On his way back to the monastery he found some Teller mines, which he took back towards a position ahead of the tanks and emplaced. Shortly afterwards Sergeant Lawrence R. Custer's tank pushed past Crew's disabled tank, drove further along the track and ran onto one of the mines, losing a track in the process. As the crew continued to engage with their machine guns, Eckel made his way back to where he knew there was a store of more mines. In the meantime, seeing the stricken tank, Crowder came forward in the Indian recce tank and rescued Custer and his assistant driver but, seeing more Germans in the area, he pulled back. Staff Sergeant John Kovak made another attempt to rescue the other two with his tank but, seeing the Germans in the area, also gave up. The

Americans then turned to rescuing Crews and his men. One of the Indian tanks pulled alongside their tank and took off two men, leaving Crews and his hull gunner to hold off against them for another 45 minutes until their rescue. Eckel returned to Custer's tank armed with two Teller mines fixed with igniters that he heaved onto the turret. At this point the last two members of its crew hastily evacuated the tank, after which it exploded, the turret being ripped off.

In the meantime, further back there were more problems for the Americans. Private Harold Hite's tank capsized in a crater near an old water tank. Two of his crew managed to escape under covering fire and were picked up by another tank. Near Lennie's capsized Sherman Sergeant Leonard E. Reese's Stuart ran into some soft ground and got stuck. Wright came forward his tank, got two men off but drove into a crater and got stuck himself. De Right managed to rescue Wright and one other in his tank but could not do anything about the others. All further attempts to rescue them failed.

The remaining tanks pulled back to the crest of the ridge overlooking Massa Albaneta where they remained under sniper and desultory fire. Barton was recalled to Madras Circus by Adye, leaving Moodie in charge of their depleted force. After exploring a number of avenues with Barton, Adye agreed that there was nothing more they could do and ordered the rest of the force to withdraw to Madras Circus, the tanks pulling out around 5.30pm. Thus ended Operation Revenge.

Oppisite above: The start of Cavendish Road was marked by this sign at the beginning of the track near Caira. (PISM)

Oppisite below: A view of Cavendish Road taken near the top of the road. The lower track branching off from it on the right was improved to take mules only. (PISM)

Corporal Rex Miller's Sherman III from C Squadron, 20th NZ Armoured Regiment slipped off the road from Caira just before the turn off to Cavendish Road. (PISM)

One of the next casualties
from C Squadron, 20th NZ
Armoured Regiment was that
of Lieutenant 'Stuffy' Hazlett,
whose Sherman III slipped
into a small ditch beside track
in the valley beyond Madras
Circus. The Germans blew it
up later. (PISM)

Shortly after Hazlett's tank capsized, Lieutenant Bill de Lautour's tank shed a track trying to climb a spur on Phantom Ridge. (PISM)

This M5A1 light tank from Company D, 760th Tank Battalion got bogged just beyond Hazlett's Sherman III. (PISM)

Lennie's tank was hit by a Panzerschreck round near Massa Albaneta, disabling one of the motors. It then slipped sideways into a crater trying to get away. (PISM)

Lieutenant John A. Crews' tank was trying to turn around when it was hit by a round from by a Panzerschreck fired by Gefrieter Kammermann and disabled. (NARA)

The next five images show Sergeant Lawrence R. Custer's tank which, after pushing past Crew's disabled tank, ran onto a mine laid by Oberleutnant Raimund Eckel. He attacked it shortly afterwards with more mines. (PISM)

While trying to get back to the saddle Private Harold Hite's tank capsized in a crater, as these four images show. (PISM)

These five images show Sergeant Leonard E. Reese's Stuart tank that got stuck in some soft ground, but when Lieutenant Chester M. Wright came forward, his tank got stuck as well. He and one crew member were rescued by Lieutenant de Right in his tank. (PISM)

The surviving tanks and crews laagered at Madras Circus overnight. Photographed at breakfast the following morning were the crew of this tank: Baird, Stillburn, 'Shorty' Shorrocks, Captain Jim Moodie and 'Digger' Grant, Moodie having been wounded by a stray piece of shrapnel whilst on watch the previous night.

Chapter Seven

Prelude to Operation Diadem

With the failure of the Third Battle, Alexander decided to focus his main effort on a broad front around Cassino in the spring, suspending all operations on the Adriatic coast. For this new offensive the American and French troops of the 5th Army were to be drawn together in the coastal sector, leaving the 8th Army responsible for the Liri Valley and Monte Cassino. To achieve this the British were to take over the defence of Cassino, allowing the New Zealanders to replace the French on Monte Cifalco and around Sant'Elia. The Poles were to take over Monte Cairo from the French and the Indians on Snakeshead Ridge.

As this rearrangement took some time 2nd NZ Division was left to garrison Cassino township for a few weeks more, taking over this role on the night of 24/25 March. The following day the New Zealand Corps was disbanded. At this point 20th NZ Armoured Regiment took over responsibility for tank support in the town. This meant maintaining tanks in three different locations. The first of these was around the Jail and involved three tanks, all of which could not be moved. Here replacement crews made their way in by foot at night and had to spend three days in them before being replaced. Because the tanks were under constant observation from above the crews could not make any external changes, even down to keeping the periscopes fixed in the same orientation. Battery charging was carried out with the main engine or the Homelight chargers, usually during an artillery barrage at night. This meant that the replacement crews had to bring fuel in with them. Crews spent the entire daylight hours inside the tanks, usually only getting out at nightfall. All activities had to be conducted inside the tank, including cooking and toileting, there being several options for the latter, the crews either using shell cases or opening up the escape hatch behind the spare driver's seat.

Early on in the occupation three tanks were based at the Convent, but this was reduced to two by the lack of cover and their crews were forced to move them inside the Convent. Once again replacement crews had to make their way in on foot at night. A further four tanks were assigned a counter-penetration role two miles to the east. At this site problems were experienced with a German anti-tank gun with a field of fire encompassing Route 6. It knocked out one tank from 20th NZ

Armoured Regiment, killing its commander, Corporal Norman Lovelock, and his gunner. Another tank from the unit slipped into a crater on the outskirts of the Botanical Gardens. Shellfire was also a constant problem for the tanks, one had its electrical system knocked out by a near miss but its crew was able to repair it on site. Another had its radiator holed on 29 March. The regiment ordered a retaliatory artillery strike on an anti-tank gun south of the Baron's Palace and in turn one of their tanks in the Convent was hit by a shell and its crew evacuated.

At the railway station the tanks were able to drive in along the now-repaired railway embankment to replace those in and around the station yards. When 19th NZ Armoured Regiment first reached the station there had been cover for six tanks. However, by 23 March shellfire had reduced the available cover and there was now only enough for four tanks. The first tanks sent in by 20th NZ Armoured Regiment came from 2 Troop under Second-Lieutenant 'Snow' Nixon but his tank was holed by an anti-tank gun and set on fire just after reaching the station yards. Nixon, his gunner and loader were wounded, the gunner dying later from his wounds.

On the night of 30/31 March a small group of paratroopers launched a surprise attack on Lieutenant Rod Eastgate's 5 Troop from B Squadron. They hit Sergeant Bill Watson's tank with a panzerschreck, climbed onto the turret, ordered the crew to open up and killed everyone in the turret when they did so. The spare driver tried to escape through the bottom of the tank but was shot and killed, the driver being captured. The paratroopers then turned their attention to Corporal Jim Boniface's tank, climbing onto it and attempting to do the same but its crew had been alerted by some infantry and swung the turret around, sweeping the paratroopers off with a barrel of their 75mm. The paratroopers were then cut down by fire from some 26th NZ Battalion soldiers in a nearby building. The paratroopers launched another attack just before dawn but Eastgate and Boniface moved their tanks over to the roundhouse and opened up on the attackers. Further support came from Sergeant J.G. Reid who raced in in support under an artillery-laid smoke screen. The attack was eventually driven off, paratrooper losses amounting to twenty-three dead and five captured. The tenure of 20th NZ Armoured Regiment continued until the 15th by which time there was only sufficient cover four two tanks at the railway station. They were then replaced by a Canadian armoured unit.

Alexander's final plans for the new offensive, Operation Diadem, called for a simultaneous attack along the whole of the Gustav Line. The CEF in the 5th Army, under Clark, were to outflank the German forces in the Liri Valley by sending his mountain troops through the Arunci Mountains and thence via Esperia and Monte d'Oro. To their left the American 2nd Corps was to advance up the Ausente Valley, to the west of Castelforte and capture the town of Santa Maria Infante. Thereafter they were to push onto the Pico-Itri lateral road, and onwards through Monte Civita and Castellonorato. The breakthrough in the Liri Valley was entrusted to the 8th Army under Lieutenant General Oliver Leese. For this the Polish Corps, under the command of Lieutenant General Wladyslaw Anders, was to dominate Route 6 by isolating Monte Cassino and ultimately capturing the monastery. Below them the British 13th Corps under Lieutenant General Sydney Kirkman were to cross the Gari River and isolate Cassino from the west. The date for the launch was set for 11 May.

As part of the preparations for this, on 19 March the Allies began an air offensive, Operation Strangle, aimed isolating the Cassino area by destroying at German road, rail and sea communications south of the Rimini–Pisa Line. At the same time they set up a deception plan aimed at fooling the Germans into thinking another seaborne invasion was being planned. Under this they began their planned redeployment of units, along with a scheme to provide relief from the line for those troops taking part in the main assault.

Though the Germans were not totally fooled by the deception plan, they did retain a strong belief that the Allies were considering another seaborne assault. Kesselring, realizing that an Allied assault on the Adriatic coast was not likely, also managed to reinforce XIV Panzerkorps around Cassino with troops from that part of the line. Nevertheless the front-line units found themselves in considerable difficulties as Kesselring had placed all his mobile divisions into his army group reserve around Rome. By 12 April they were also of the view that a major attack was not likely in the near future to the extent that the XIV Panzerkorps commander, General Fridolin von Senger und Etterlin, decided to go on thirty days' leave on that date. The Germans had also undertaken a reorganization of units of their own, which was still not complete when Diadem was eventually launched.

Lieutenant 'Snow' Nixon's Sherman III was knocked out and set on fire by an anti-tank gun shortly after arriving at the railway station on 23 March. (20th Armoured Battalion and Regimental Archives; Frank White)

On 25 March Corporal Norman Lovelock's tank from 3 Troop A Squadron, 20th NZ Armoured Regiment was knocked out outside the Convent by an anti-tank gun, killing Lovelock and Trooper Lester Fowler. (ATL)

On 26 March this tank from 20th NZ Armoured Regiment slipped off Pasquale Road on its way into Cassino. (ATL)

Outside the area of fighting this crewman from 20th NZ Armoured Regiment lounges by his Sherman.

This Sherman III from 20 NZ Armoured Regiment slipped into a crater between the Convent and the Chiesa di San Antonio sometime towards the end of March. Note No. 13 Tank in the distance beside the Chiesa Di San Antonio. (NARA)

After the fighting came to an end in Cassino the 20th NZ Armoured Regiment found and recovered this T2 Armoured Recovery Vehicle that the Americans had abandoned in the flooded ground of the Rapido Valley during the fighting in January. (ECPAD)

While 18th NZ Armoured Regiment was in reserve its squadrons took turns to undertake fire-support missions on Cassino along a gun line behind Monte Trocchio. (Pat Gourdie)

New Zealand tank crews were sometimes called upon to man these Canadian tanks on the Caira-Terelle road. (Des Tomkies)

'Blastaway' ran onto mines on the Caira–Terelle road after undertaking a fire mission towards Cassino. (Des Tomkies)

A 28th (Maori) Battalion Universal Carrier on its way up to Terelle. (ATL)

One tank that featured many times in books and documentaries on Cassino was Lieutenant Bob McCowan's from RHQ of 19th Armoured Regiment; McCowan second from right on the turret. The still and movie images were actually shot in Mignano with 11th Platoon of 22nd NZ Motor Battalion providing the infantry. (Harry Hopping)

At least one action shot of McCowan's tank was taken from the same wrecked building. (Harry Hopping)

McCowan and some infantry taking a break at his tank during the filming at Mignano. (ATL)

New Zealand troops inspect two of their Sherman IIIs that ended up in a ditch in Cassino. (ATL)

Chapter Eight

Diadem – the Coastal Sector

At 11.00pm on the night of 11/12 May the guns and howitzers of 5th and 8th Armies opened up on the German positions, the bombardment continuing until the early hours of the following morning. After that had ceased, in the American sector 85th Division in the south went in against the Germans holding a feature known as the S-Ridge, Colle San Martino and the Domenico Ridge, while 88th Division, to their right, pushed north from Minturno towards Santa Maria Infante. For 85 Division this soon turned into a struggle but the division did manage to gain a foothold on the lower slopes of the Domenico Ridge before getting pinned down, something that also happened to the battalions that managed to reach the crest of the S-Ridge. Throughout the rest of the day they fought off a number of counter-attacks, so by nightfall had very little to show for their efforts.

Further north 88th Division's attack towards Santa Maria Infante encountered strong opposition right from the time they left their start line at the Minturno cemetery. Under intense machine-gun fire their attack soon broke up into a series of small-unit actions. One small force of 100 men, after assembling at the cemetery, managed to find a break in the defences and reached the outskirts of Tame. Another company to the right got to the crest of the ridge, along which they were to advance, but were forced back by machine-gun fire.

Around 3.00am a request was sent back to 760th Tank Battalion for support but they had run into strong opposition themselves. So it was not until mid-morning that a platoon of tanks from Company C under First Lieutenant Eugene E. Gleissner managed to get up to the cemetery. Gleissner then set off with three tanks but his ran onto a mine and was disabled. Some liaison officers from the infantry came forward and ordered Staff Sergeant Pinckney D. Upchurch's tank forward but it too ran onto a mine, blocking the road in the process. The third tank then tried to move forward but also ran onto a mine. The infantry sent out a request for another tank platoon but that did not arrive for several hours, leaving them pinned down by intense machine-gun fire. In the meantime the divisional mine platoon cleared the mines along the road. Thus, when a second platoon of tanks from Company C arrived they were able to advance several hundred yards along the road and eliminate a number of German machine-gun nests, losing three tanks in the process to anti-tank guns in Santa Maria Infante. Around 3.00pm a platoon from Company A under 1st Lieutenant Clinton F. Des Jardins arrived and took out some more German strongpoints, before pushing on down the road and knocking out a self-propelled gun. Further down the road, Des Jardins' tank was knocked out and set on fire by another German self-propelled gun. Two more American tanks were knocked out shortly afterwards.

Around sunrise that day Company B from 760th Tank Battalion set off from Tufo along a narrow Jeep trail down a wadi in an attempt to find another way to get up to the infantry around Santa Maria Infante. While there were difficulties negotiating this route, the main problem occurred further down where a number of tanks became stuck in the boggy ground beside the Reali Creek. Two tanks from one platoon later ran onto mines and were disabled. The company then spent the next day trying to recover their tanks, though it took the assistance of two armoured dozers from the engineers after their own T2 recovery vehicle got stuck.

On 13 May 85th Division took Colle San Martino only to be ordered to consolidate on what they had taken, to allow 88th Division make the main effort on the right. Having secured Monte Damino 88th Division pushed on towards Santa Maria Infante capturing some hills above it with relative ease as French successes in the Arunci Mountains had forced the Germans to withdraw their troops across the Ausonia defile. The following morning, after taking Santa Maria Infante, and joining up with Company B, 760th Tank Battalion, they moved on beyond the town. Here the tanks spotted some German tanks on the Ausonia Road, forcing them to scatter behind buildings or into ravines, only to pull out later, allowing the combined force onto the Ausonia Road. Good progress was made until they neared Route 7 where the Germans blew a bridge over a small creek, forcing the American tanks to find cover as they came under fire from 88mm guns and self-propelled guns on the road leading to Spigno. Eventually a tank dozer appeared and prepared a crossing over the creek, allowing them to push on and join up with a column of tanks from 756th Tank Battalion.

Around 4.00pm the two armoured columns joined up and attacked Formia. Little resistance was met at first but when they forded the first stream and continued through the olive grove and farm buildings they came under intense direct fire. Sergeant Fred J. Shumaker's tank took a direct hit but only he managed to bail out before it burst into flames. Sergeant Alva J. Morgan's tank was hit and set on fire, wounding him and killing the gunner. Some of the crew was rescued but the rest died in the tank. A further six tanks were also knocked out, one of which also caught fire. As the sun was going down the tanks pulled back leaving those that had caught fire still glowing red hot. They discovered that they had overrun a few Germans in a cluster of houses. These they shot up in the near darkness, driving the Germans out.

On the afternoon of 14 May a battalion of infantry from 85th Division, along with two platoons of 756th Tank Battalion, set out to clear the high ground before Castellonorato. At the Capo d'Acqua stream the tanks were forced to halt because the engineers had been unable to complete a ford after they came under artillery fire. In the end 1st Lieutenant William M. Hammer, frustrated by the delays, ordered his tank forward but as it eased its way into the water the bank started to give way so his driver gunned the engine as the tank dropped into the river and got it safely to the other side. Following his lead the rest of his platoon and that of 2nd Lieutenant Roland V. Hunter's platoon also crossed successfully. Both platoons then fanned out as they ascended the slope capturing some Germans along with an anti-tank gun, destroying two other anti-tank guns and capturing a further twenty Germans on the crest of the ridge. This forced the rest of the Germans to pull back to Castellonorato but when the tanks nosed over the ridge they came under intense fire and were forced to pull back behind the crest where they were joined by a company of infantry around sundown.

The following day Castellonorato was bombed and strafed by fighter-bombers. The Americans then pushed into it, securing it after several hours street fighting. At this point the weight of their advance shifted towards the 85th Division's sector along the coast with the view to outflanking the town of Formia some 6km further forward. At the same time 88th Division, with two companies of 760th Tank Battalion in support, set off along Route 7 aided by two British cruisers and US Navy destroyers. Several pillboxes and anti-tank guns were destroyed in the process along with three self-propelled guns. Formia was finally entered on 18 May.

A M4A1 Sherman from 760th Tank Battalion passes the Minturno cemetery. The Sherman III on the side of the road was most probably knocked out during the British attack in January 1944. (NARA)

As this column of Shermans from 760th Tank Battalion moved up towards Santa Maria Infante on 14 May they passed by tanks knocked out two days previously. (NARA)

This Semovente in Santa Maria Infante was knocked out during the fighting for the town. (NARA)

On the morning of 12 May Company B, 760th Tank Battalion set off to find an alternative route to Tufo. (NARA)

They soon found themselves heading down a narrow Jeep trail. (NARA)

At times the crews had to dismount to assist the passage of their tanks along the trail. (NARA)

Lower down the company ran into a grassy meadow. (NARA)

When the tanks reached the Reali creek at the bottom their troubles were far from over. Several of them got stuck in the creek and the marshy ground, as shown in the following five images. (NARA)

Worst still, the T2 ARV
that accompanied
them capsized in the
soft going. (NARA)

Some of the tanks found a way past the stuck tanks and managed to continue their journey, though the going was still difficult. (NARA)

The other tanks and the T2 ARV were not recovered until the next day when the Americans sent down an armoured bulldozer. (NARA)

An American reconnaissance unit prepares to depart from the town of Formia on 18 May. (NARA)

An American soldier inspects a Marder III Ausf M from 1 Kompanie, Panzerjäger-Abteilung 194 from 94 Infanterie-Division captured during the fighting for Castelonorato. (NARA)

Shermans from 760th Tank Battalion moving up through Formia in preparation for the continuation of the advance along the coast towards Gaeta and Itri. (NARA)

Chapter Nine

Diadem – the Arunci Mountains

The main objective of the CEF was the Monte Maio massif and this was entrusted to 2éme Division d'Infanterie Marocains. To the south of them 4éme Régiment de Tirailleurs Tunisiens, backed up by armour, was assigned to the capture of Castelforte. On the northern flank 1ére Division de Marche d'Infanterie was to drive northwards along the western bank of the Garigliano before swinging to the left to mop up the south bank of the Liri River.

As with the Americans, the French attack was preceded by the same preliminary bombardment, except in the Moroccan sector, where, in an attempt to surprise the defenders, no barrage was fired at all. Despite this, and the silent advance of the Moroccans, the German defenders were quick to react and put down a strong fusillade of machine-gun fire. While one battalion made good progress, taking the summit of Monte Falto, the others struggled to move forward.

Things went better the next day. The Moroccans launched their attack at 3.15am and made good progress as they proceeded further into the Arunci mountains. Around 8.00am they beat off a determined attack launched by the Germans when the Moroccans threw in their sole reserve formation. Monte Feuci fell around 11.15am and from that position they realized that Monte Maio, the highest mountain in the range, was unoccupied. By 3.00pm it was theirs and from this position they were able to bring down fire onto some German troops on the plateau below, driving them off.

For the attack on Castelforte on 12 April the Tunisians had the support of some M10 tank destroyers from 7éme Régiment de Chasseurs d'Afrique and Shermans from US 755th Tank Battalion. Here they also benefited from the failure of the Germans to occupy the ground in front of Castelforte. The Tunisian attack kicked off along two lines of advance from San Sebastino and San Lorenzo, making good progress over this ground. By nightfall some tanks from 755th Tank Battalion had penetrated as far as the square in Castelforte. The following day the Tunisians pushed further into Castelforte, clearing it house by house, their men sometimes crawling under the bellies of their tank destroyers. With the town finally cleared around midday their armoured group pushed on towards Coreno and Ausonia.

On the northern flank that day 3éme Régiment de Spahis Marocains and 757th

Tank Battalion lost a number of tanks after they ran into a minefield. This forced them to halt their attack near Conventi. Fortunately the success of their mountain troops the following day had ramifications for them, as the elimination of flanking fire from the mountains to their left led to a considerable improvement in progress along their route. On the road to Sant'Ambrogio one of the Spahis' troops of M5A1 tanks charged straight down the road towards a roadblock. Though they lost two tanks to an anti-tank gun, they managed to drive off the gunners and other troops with machine-gun fire. Two more tanks were lost to panzerfausts but the tank crews carried on dismounted until more tanks arrived. Sant'Ambrogio fell that evening and by dusk they had reached the outskirts of Sant'Apollinare. This they cleared of Germans on the morning of 14 April. Beyond there they ran into a hastily thrown-together battlegroup of German infantry and reconnaissance units that brought them to an untimely halt until the Germans were forced to pull back to San Giorgio thanks to an outflanking movement by the Moroccans in the mountains to the south. The French quickly closed up but were unable to make any progress initially. However, San Giorgio finally fell to them late in the afternoon next day.

On 14 May the Algerians came within striking distance of Ausonia but were held up by another battlegroup the Germans had assembled. That same day, with their sights set on Esperia, two battalions of Algerian troops were sent through the mountains to the east of that town, securing this by noon. Another battalion was sent up the road until it was checked by fire from La Bastia. Eventually, on the night of 14/15 May some Moroccan troops took a mountain behind Esperia, forcing the Germans to give up Ausonia and begin a full-scale retreat, leaving a only small group behind in Esperia.

Things then turned from bad to worse for the Germans in Esperia on 17 May when a Piper Club spotter plane discovered a German column from 71 Infanterie-Division withdrawing from the town along the narrow road leading down towards Monticelli. The French responded immediately with a concentrated artillery barrage that destroyed some fifty armoured vehicles, guns and other vehicles and all but wiped out the column. The Algerians then launched their attack on Esperia itself but got involved in a six-hour battle with the remnants of 71 Infanterie-Division and other units. The Germans exacted their revenge that afternoon when the French attempted to push down the road towards Monticelli. Being still in possession of Monte d'Oro, the Germans were able to bring down a heavy mortar bombardment on the French column. This brought the advance to a halt and forced the French to fall back to Esperia until they could secure Monte d'Oro. This cleared they were able to continue their thrust on towards Sant'Olivia, reaching it on 18 May.

M4 Shermans from Company B, 755th Tank Battalion prepare to fire on Castelforte on 11 May. (NARA)

French-manned half-tracks crossing the Garigliano River. (NARA)

French muleteers on the road from San Lorenzo to Castelforte pass a knocked-out StuG III lost during the fighting in January. (NARA)

Shermans from Company C, 755th Tank Battalion after entering the village of Santi Cosmi e Damiano on 12 May. (NARA)

Company C, 755th Tank Battalion along with a M10 tank destroyer from 7éme Régiment de Chasseurs d'Afrique strike out for Castelforte. (NARA)

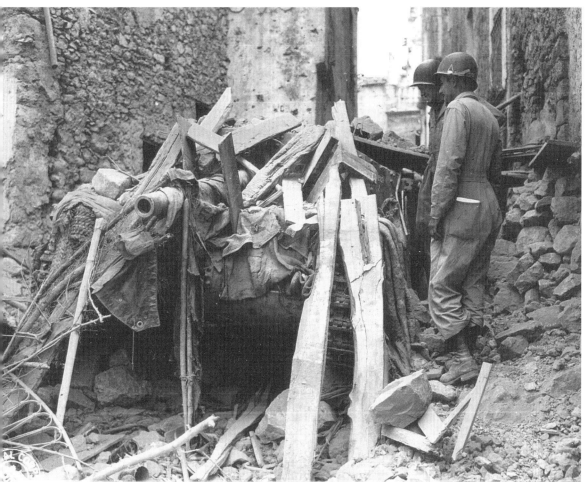

This Semovente M42 da 75/34 from Panzerjäger-Abteilung 171, 71 Infanterie-Division was found buried under rubble in Santi Cosmi e Damiano. (NARA)

An M8 Howitzer Motor Carriage from 3éme Régiment de Spahis Algeriens on the road into Santi Cosmi e Damiano. (NARA)

This M4 Sherman from 755th Tank Battalion was knocked on the outskirts of Castelforte during the attack on 12 May. (NARA)

An M10 tank destroyer from 7éme Régiment de Chasseurs d'Afrique pushes past a wrecked StuG III in the town of Castelforte. (ECPAD)

An M10 tank destroyer of 7éme Régiment de Chasseurs d'Afrique at the eastern end of Castelforte. (ECPAD)

Another Semovente M42 from Panzerjäger-Abteilung 171, 71 Infanterie-Division was found in a cellar of a house in Castelforte. (NARA)

The crews of two M5A1 Stuarts and an M4 Sherman from 755th Tank Battalion take a break in Coreno after its capture by the French on 14 May. (NARA)

M4 Shermans of 755th Tank Battalion accompanying the Dodelier Detachment pass through the Ausonia Defile on 15 May. (Pierre Ichac)

A M5A1 Stuart of 1er Escadron of the Fusiliers Marins passing through Sant'Apollinare on 14 May 1944 after its capture. (NARA)

M4A1 Shermans from 755th Tank Battalion in laager between Vallemaio and Sant'Apollinare. (NARA)

A M5A1 Stuart of 577th Tank Battalion on the move in the Liri Valley. (NARA)

M4 Shermans and T2 ARV of the 757th Tank Battalion and an M3 scout car belonging to 22ème Battalion de Marche Nord-Africain in San Giorgio after its capture on 15 May. (Real War Pictures)

A French M5A1 at speed in the Liri Valley. (NARA)

The French took Ausonia on 15 May, this M10 tank destroyer of the 7ème Regiment de Chasseurs d'Afrique passing through later. (NARA)

Panzerjäger-Abteilung 171, 71 Infanterie-Division was forced to abandon this Semovente M42 da 75/18 in Esperia on 17 May 1944. (NARA)

The French pushed this Marder III Ausf H from Panzerjäger-Abteilung 171 off the Esperia-Monticelli road after destroying a retreating column from 71 Infanterie-Division on 17 May. (NARA)

Another victim of the French artillery fire on a column from 71 Infanterie-Division near Esperia was this Semovente M42 da 75/34 from 2 Kompanie, Panzerjäger-Abteilung 171. (NARA)

Not all vehicles were pushed off the Esperia-Monticelli road immediately: this Sd.Kfz. 251/10 Ausf C from 90 Panzergrenadier-Division was one of them. (Lee Archer)

... later it was. (NARA)

Further down the road the French found another Marder III Ausf. H from 1 Kompanie, Panzerjäger-Abteilung 171. (ECPAD)

French troops moving onto Monticelli from Esperi pass another victim of the artillery barrage, a Sd.Kfz. 251/3 Ausf. C from 90 Panzergrenadier-Division. (NARA)

A M4 Sherman from 755th Tank Battalion takes up position behind a house in Monticelli after its capture. (Real War Pictures)

Chapter Ten

Diadem – the Liri Valley

One of the lessons learned from the fatal attack by the Texans in January 1944 was the need to establish bridges for tanks across the Gari River as soon as possible after the infantry had secured a bridgehead. With this in mind the plans of the 13th Corps commander, Lieutenant General Sidney Kirkman, were for three bridges in 4th Division's sector to the north ('Amazon', 'Blackwater' and 'Congo') and four in 8th Indian Division's sector in the south ('Cardiff', 'London', 'Oxford' and 'Plymouth'). 'Of these 'Plymouth' was to be launched in quite a unique way using a method devised by Captain Tony Kingsmill, the Commander Royal Engineers of the Canadian Calgary Regiment. His proposal called for the pre-assembly of a Bailey bridge, which was then to be manoeuvred into position by two Sherman tanks. One tank, known as the Carrier, had its turret removed and replaced by a steel I-beam with four rocking rollers to support the bridge. With the Bailey bridge balanced on the Carrier tank, the bridge was to be pushed across the river by a second Sherman known as the Pusher. Once the bridge had extended far enough over the river the Carrier was to drive down into the river thus allowing the bridge to drop into place. The crew was then to bail out of the Carrier and swim ashore.

When the attack was launched on 11 May results were mixed in the 4th Division sector. The two assaulting battalions from 10th Brigade managed to get across, form up and take their objectives. In contrast one battalion from 28th Brigade to their south got lost in fog while moving up to the Gari River and then the other got mixed up with them. By the time they had crossed the river the fog had lifted and they were hit by strong defensive fire. This forced them to dig in where they had landed, in some cases occupying only a thin strip of land along the riverbank. As a result no progress was made on any of their bridges, the engineers coming under heavy artillery fire when they tried to work on them.

Aided by some thick mist on the river the Indians launched their assault at 11.45pm. on 11 May. The majority of infantry from 17th Indian Brigade made it over the river without great difficulty but then many got confused in the mist and became dispersed or lost. The fog also blinded their artillery observers and the tanks of the Three Rivers Regiment, who were supposed to provide direct fire support. Their reserve battalions were then sent over, among them 1st Battalion 5th Gurkhas, one company of which had been detailed to attack Sant'Angelo in Theodice but two platoons got lost, so their attempt to take it on the first day failed. In the south 19th Indian Brigade ran into more difficulties. After crossing the river the assaulting battalions ran into heavy defensive fire that plunged one battalion into a savage firefight and drove another back to the river where they were forced to huddle in the water until they were rescued.

Despite this the two Indian brigades had gained sufficient ground to enable their engineers to begin work on their bridges. The first to be completed was 'Oxford' and by morning it was ready for the tanks of B Squadron, the Ontario Regiment, that is until three Stuart tanks of the Three Rivers Regiment recce squadron nosed their way down to the bridge. There the lead tank dropped into a crater and bellied on a Teller mine that ripped open its floor plate and temporarily blocked the path. When B Squadron of the Ontario Regiment eventually crossed over they were forced to turn south towards the site of 'Plymouth' because of some mines blocking the way to their assigned objective, the Sant-Angelo-San Apollinare road. Then, on orders to retrace their steps, 4 Troop shooting up some machine-gun posts before departing. Eight of their tanks became bogged on crossing some open ground, leaving the rest of the squadron to link up with 1st Battalion 5th Gurkhas.

The next bridge to be launched on the night of 11/12 May was 'Plymouth' but after the bridging convoy set off along the white-taped corridor for their assigned bridge site, one of the trucks carrying bridging material straying off the track in the fog and overturned. Then the Carrier tank swung off the path forcing Trooper Ian Seymour, its radio operator, to retrace their track ruts back to the main route until he got lost in the dark and had to take shelter in a crater. At this point Kingsmill ordered the tank driver, Trooper George MacLean, to rev the tank engine and, in doing so, guide Seymour back. Though this had the unfortunate effect of bringing down a barrage of mortar fire from the Germans, it did enable Kingsmill to lead the Carrier tank back to the main route on foot, where they set out once more for the river. By now, however, they were badly behind schedule and when dawn came the engineers were still assembling the bridge. Worse still, the fog that had kept their position obscured for a time it was now starting to clear under the blazing sun. A smoke-generation team was brought up but it could only maintain cover for so long. Fortunately, by the time visibility had extended out to 200 yards the bridge was ready so the Pusher and Carrier tanks with the Bailey bridge mounted set out for the river. Fifteen yards from the river Kingsmill ordered the Carrier tank to halt and the Pusher tank to continue advancing, gradually extending the bridge out across the river. When the bridge was halfway across Kingsmill realized that the Carrier tank was sinking into the mud and the bank was starting to cave in under its weight. At that point he ordered MacLean to drive the Carrier tank into the river, only for it to progress a short way into the river before it became mired in the mud and then the bridge dropped with a crash onto the other side. Though no damage was done the bridge was now balanced finely on top of the Carrier tank like a see-saw; its entrance resting on the eastern bank of the river with the other end on the western bank some 3ft off the ground. At this point Kingsmill jumped out and swam to the shore, followed by Seymour, who was about to rescue MacLean when his hatch opened and he too escaped.

The first troops across 'Plymouth' bridge were actually Germans. Kingsmill spotted three of them burst from a nearby thicket of rushes, run past some engineers and dash across the bridge before anyone could do anything about them. They were followed soon after by 1 Troop, A Squadron from the Calgary Regiment under the command of Lieutenant Al Wells and it was now that the peculiarity of the bridge placement became apparent. As Wells' tank reached the pivot point over the Carrier the bridge tipped downwards coming to rest on the other bank allowing his tank to drive off without incident. Once off, the bridge swung back down allowing his troop corporal's tank to drive onto the bridge, and it too made it across without incident. The problem came when the next tank under Sergeant Rolly Marchant drove onto the bridge. This time it did not drop when they reached the pivot point, as Lieutenant Jim Quinn's tank had driven onto the bridge behind him. Instead when Marchant's tank reached the other end it dropped 3ft to the ground with a solid crash that shorted out the tank's electrical system. The bridge, now free of Marchant's tank, pivoted as before and Quinn's tank made it over without further incident. But now the bridge had to be closed as the engineers discovered that the ramps on the western bank had slipped and needed to be replaced. To deal with this Kingsmill and MacLean went back for some replacements in a spare Carrier but both were wounded while they were unloading the ramps after they returned. This further delayed bridge re-opening until later that evening but only for Jeeps. Nevertheless, though B Squadron of the Calgary Regiment were unable to cross 'Plymouth' that day, they were able to put down sufficient supporting fire for the Indians to enable them to secure a foothold just across the San Apollinare-Sant'Angelo road.

Wells' troop and Quinn's tank were now in the narrow bridgehead held by the Indian troops. Observing some German machine-gun fire coming from an embankment ahead of them, they engaged this with their machine guns, while Marchant's gunner lobbed over a few delayed-fuse high explosive shells. They then set out for the San Apollinare–Sant'Angelo road to meet up with the Argyll and Sutherland Highlanders, taking up a position in some brush on the outskirts of Panaccioni. While camouflaging their tanks with brush they spotted some German activity around a large building that they took to be a headquarters and then saw a number of infantry and tracked vehicles heading towards to San Angelo. Restraining from firing themselves Wells called fire down upon the latter, leaving several vehicles burning. Their luck eventually ran out when they were spotted among the trees by some German infantry who initially gave them a wave, thinking they were friendly until it became apparent that they had realized their mistake and then the Canadian tanks opened up, killing most of them. Having now revealed their presence the tanks began firing on whatever targets they had observed in the town but this only brought down mortar and artillery fire on them. Eventually, with still no sign of their own infantry, they were ordered to withdraw.

At 'Oxford' bridge, with B Squadron of the Ontario Regiment across, C Squadron was scheduled to cross next but now had to take their place behind another unit, C Squadron of the Calgary Regiment, that was urgently required by 3rd Battalion 8th Punjabi Regiment and was on its way up from 'Plymouth' bridge. When the Calgary tanks did arrive they ran into more problem. Corporal Bill McWithey's tank, in the lead, got stuck in the muddy ground 100 yards from the river. With no engineers around to retrieve it, Lieutenant Al Cawsey inched his tank out of the marked path and, with his spare driver, guiding the tank on foot, successfully negotiated their way to the front of McWithey's tank, narrowly avoiding three mines in the process. Once in front they hooked a towrope to McWithey's tank and pulled it out. The pair of them then set off over the bridge leaving the rest of the squadron behind, the road being too badly chewed up for them to use.

Beyond the bridge Cawsey and McWithey joined up with the Punjabis only to find that they had suffered heavy casualties during the night, the company commander having only ten men out of his original eighty that had crossed the river earlier. Cawsey was advised that the tanks would have to operate without infantry support and when he contacted his squadron commander, Major Don Taylor, he was ordered to proceed to their original objective, Panaccioni, where the rest of the squadron would join him later. Just before setting off McWithey spotted a German self-propelled gun lining up against them. Cawsey's gunner opened fire and hit the self-propelled gun with his first round, forcing its crew to bail out. McWithey then cut the crew down with machine-gun fire as they tried to escape. A little while later Cawsey's tank came upon an assault gun astride a sunken track, narrowly avoiding hitting it in the process. He lobbed a grenade into its open cupola, while McWithey's tank fired an AP round into it shortly afterwards, knocking it out. Only one crewman escaped from the assault gun and he climbed onto the back of Cawsey's tank but when the two tanks came under an intense artillery barrage the German attempted to climb inside. Cawsey ducked inside the turret, after which McWithey machine-gunned the German off the back of Cawsey's tank.

Driving through the barrage unscathed they ran into another self-propelled gun some 250 yards away, which Cawsey's gunner knocked out, overrunning and destroying a 75mm Pak forty minutes later. Beyond there they reached a small hill to the south of Panaccioni, where, still without infantry support, Cawsey radioed back to Taylor for further instructions. The news was grim, 'Oxford' had been put out of action and it would be several hours before the squadron could join them. Taylor ordered them to stay put and call in artillery support if and when needed. Taylor eventually managed to get a few more of his squadron over the river and after joining up with Cawsey and McWithey proceeded to shoot up Panaccioni until nightfall when they pulled back to the Punjabi positions to refuel and replenish their ammunition. There they were joined by Quinn and Well's troop. The following morning (13 May) they finally learned their infantry, the Argyll and Sutherland Highlanders, had been thrown back from the western bank of the river during the attack on the night of 11/12 May. Those that had survived had been forced to huddle in the water along the bank until the following night when the Highlanders finally successfully crossed the river, linking up around dawn with A Squadron of the Calgary Regiment.

When the mist did clear mid-morning on 13 May 1st Battalion 12th Frontier Force Rifles set off with the ten remaining tanks of C Squadron of the Ontario Regiment toward Sant'Angelo, the attack being preceded by a five-minute artillery barrage. After fighting their way through a number of machine-gun posts the infantry broke into a cemetery 1,000 yards south of the village and overcame the German defenders in a short but furious piece of hand-to-hand fighting. Two troops from B Squadron then set off along the San Apollinare-Sant'Angelo road only to discover that the Germans had blown a bridge over a small creek. One tank attempted to cross the creek but became bogged, prompting a radio request for bridging equipment. In the meantime Corporal Lawrence Toye found a way across the stream and struck out for Sant'Angelo where he found the Gurkhas pinned down in shell holes before the village. Without hesitation he drove towards the village, machine guns blazing, the Gurkhas rising up and following close behind him. Once inside he knocked out a PzKpfw IV in a rubble-filled basement. Sergeant John Stobbard then drove up in his tank and together they worked their way through the village until Toye ran out of 75mm ammunition. Later that evening, the bridge over the creek finally complete, the rest of their squadron joined them in the village. The Gurkhas, and two tanks then set off towards the Platform, another German strong point 200m to the north-east, its garrison choosing to surrender to them. By nightfall they and the Gurkhas had penetrated 1,000 yards beyond village.

Further south, B Squadron of the Calgary Regiment, under the command of Major Frederick Richie, crossed the Gari river and joined up with 6/13 Royal

Frontier Force Rifles just short of the San Apollinare-Sant'Angelo road from where they set off towards Panaccioni. On reaching the village they worked together eliminating various strongpoints, the infantry pin-pointing these with tracer fire from their Brens. They then pushed on towards the next ridge, losing one tank to an anti-tank gun on the way in. B Squadron responded by saturating the area with high explosive, forcing the Germans to abandon their positions and flee. With this secure C Squadron and 3rd Punjabi Regiment struck out at midday for a road junction to the northwest of the village but came under heavy fire from machine guns and anti-tank guns. Two German self-propelled guns were sighted as they neared the road junction, both of which were knocked out by the Canadians. A third self-propelled gun then hove into sight, knocking out a Canadian tank before it was itself destroyed. An hour later the road junction was secure and they were rewarded with the sight of a long line of German transport heading westwards out of Pignataro. Around 5.30pm two troops from the squadron supported the Royal Frontier Force Rifles's attack on Panaccioni but after a short stiff resistance they swept into the town where the defence collapsed, 130 or so prisoners being taken.

Though very little progress had been made on 4th Division's front during the first day of the attack they had managed to hold onto their narrow bridgehead across the river. What was really needed was tank support and for that the British decided to concentrate their effort on 'Amazon' bridge. Around 5.00pm on the night of 13 May 225th Field Company started work on its approaches and, despite being under machine-gun fire, had it ready two and a half hours later. At this point 7th Field Company arrived and started unloading their bridging equipment. As the night progressed German fire on them intensified, a situation that was not helped by the arrival of C Squadron, 17th/21st Lancers. Fortunately, one of the engineers managed to stop the lead tank some 200m from the bridge as noise of the tanks was attracting more fire. By 4.00 a.m., the bridge was complete and the engineers started to push it towards the river until the engine in their one remaining bulldozer seized, its radiator and sump pierced by machine-gun fire. At that point someone remembered the tanks, raced back and persuaded Lieutenant Wayne in the lead tank to assist. Within a short space of time the bridge was in place and Lancers proceeded across. From there they drove onto the Pioppeto stream, where their scissors-bridging tank was knocked out. Undeterred, Lieutenant David Newberry and his troop from A Squadron cut down some trees, built a log bridge over the marshy ground, pushing on until they reached the Hampshires around dusk.

With the Lancers safely across the British then set about reinforcing the bridgehead with 6th Black Watch, 2nd Royal Fusiliers and tanks of 2nd Lothians and Border Horse. The Black Watch and A Squadron swung to the south but were unable to cross the Pioppeto Stream because of the loss of the bridging tank.

Instead they followed the northern bank of the stream westwards, until reaching Point 69 where they dug in. C Squadron of the Lothians accompanied the Royal Fusiliers as far as Point 41, where the Fusiliers also dug in. The Lothians sent 1 Troop forward and into a sunken road, only to run into two German tanks when they emerged from cover. Before they could engage the German tanks one their own tanks was knocked out by an anti-tank gun. In the resulting engagement both of the two surviving Lothian's tanks destroyed the German tanks, only to succumb later that afternoon when the Germans launched a counter-attack.

Around 2.00pm 2nd Duke of Cornwall's Light Infantry, with support from 17th/21st Lancers, overran the Fallschirm-MG-Bataillon at Point 63, taking 100 prisoners and forcing the rest to retreat to the south-west. To the south of them 6th Royal West Kents and other elements of the Lothians and Border Horse struck out for the Cassino-Sant'Angelo road and by the end of the day had come within a mile of Sant'Angelo itself, having come in from behind several strongpoints overlooking the river in the process.

Morning mist covered the ground when the 13th Corps attack was launched on the 14th. In the Indian Division sector C Squadron of the Three Rivers Regiment crossed over the Gari via 'Oxford' bridge and joined up with infantry from 3rd Battalion 15th Punjabis. The combined force then set off in the direction of a series of low hills in the vicinity of Sant'Angelo known as the Horseshoe, until heavy defensive fire forced the infantry to ground, leaving the tanks to forge on ahead. Time and time again the tanks had to retreat and then go forward again, two being lost to mines and one to an anti-tank gun, until they were finally relieved that evening by B Squadron and the Royal West Kent Regiment. To the south the Ontario Regiment and the Argyll and Sutherland Highlanders cleared the last Germans out of a pocket bounded by the Liri and Gari rivers. Confusion reigned on Indian right flank, after C Squadron of the Ontario Regiment got mixed up with tanks from 26th Armoured Brigade, forcing a delay in the launch of the attack. Once underway they and 1st Royal Fusiliers ran into strong opposition supported by numerous anti-tank guns, though the latter were easily dealt with for no loss by C Squadron. B Squadron and 1/5 Gurkhas set off mid-morning and ran straight into a sizeable counter-attack, losing one tank in the process. On sighting a force of fifty Germans forming up around some farmhouses they were forced to fall back while the area was pounded by artillery. They then renewed their advance, reaching their objective around midday.

Kirkman's plans for 14 May had originally called for the commitment of 78th Division but it had only managed to get one battalion across so this was postponed until the next day. Instead 4th Division was ordered to continue its advance to allow it to conform to the dispositions of the Indians. On the left C Squadron of the

Lothians and Border Horse supported 2nd Battalion 4th Hampshires in their advance but were eventually reduced to six operational tanks in the resulting attack. They had to be relieved by a squadron from the 17th/21st Lancers, while in the centre the Lothians and the Black Watch soon became involved in six hours of gruesome fighting that led to their being relieved by the 16th/5th Lancers that evening.

On the right the attack by B Squadron of the Lothians and 1st Royal West Kents came under fire from a German strongpoint in Massa Vertechi. This task was entrusted to the 2nd Battalion/4th Hampshires with support from B Squadron, 19th NZ Armoured Regiment, the latter having crossed the Gari by way of 'Congo' bridge earlier that morning. Crossing the Pioppeto stream proved problematic, as a scissors bridge over it was in poor shape having been hit earlier in the day, and it collapsed under the weight of the first tank from 6 Troop when it was only halfway over, tipping the tank into the stream. The second tank failed to jump the stream and the third one rolled over onto its side when it attempted to climb the opposite bank. Eventually 8 Troop crossed the stream further down on a temporary bridge made of green willow logs. On reaching Massa Vertechi they found that the Hampshires had gone to ground after their first attempt but they soon rose up and took the strongpoint with their support and some from a few tanks on the other side of the stream.

There was a further change in to Kirkman's plans at this stage thanks to the failure of the Polish attack on the Cassino massif. Now 78th Division was to push further up the Liri Valley and use it to isolate Monte Cassino, though little progress was made. The Germans were still holding the start line for 78th Division and, though this was eventually cleared later that day, the division was experiencing problems bringing their other battalions across because of damage to the approaches to the bridges.

Better progress was made in the south by the Indians. The attack by the Three Rivers Regiment succeeded in a spectacular fashion when their commander threw the entire battalion into a wild cavalry-like charge that saw them cut the Cassino–Pignataro road. To the north of them B Squadron of the Calgary Regiment with the 6th Battalion 13th Royal Frontier Force Rifles secured a ridge overlooking the town of Pignataro itself. That evening they and the tanks worked their way around to the southern outskirts and fought their way in clearing it slowly house by house and by 11.00pm had reported it clear of Germans.

On 16 May the Canadians took over the attack from the Indians, their Royal Canadian Regiment with Churchills from 142nd Royal Armoured Regiment, passing through Indian lines that morning. Two hours later they succeeded in cutting the Pignataro–San Giorgio road but could make no further progress despite several attempts. To their right the Hastings and Prince Edward Regiment entered Pignataro itself only to find the Indians still in a fierce struggle to clear the town. They eventually pushed on beyond the village, running into a party of Germans at a crossroads where a short firefight ensued before the Germans disengaged.

Concurrently with this 78th Division launched its assault on the Cassino–Pignataro road, initially making good progress as they advanced across a series of ridges and hummocks. As the attack progressed the London Irish Rifles came up against German troops holed up in farm buildings en route and the pace of their advance started to flag. By the time they reached the village of Sinagoga all of the 17th/21st Lancers' tanks had been knocked out by 88mms to the rear of the village. They took the village but their leading platoon was all but cut down by defensive fire. The Lancashire Fusiliers, to their right, ran into similar problems but reached a ridge adjacent to Sinagoga without losing too many casualties but the tanks from 17th/21st Lancers were hampered by the close wooded country and blocked from crossing the skyline of a ridge by the German defenders on the other side. In the end the Fusiliers had to deal with a counter-attack backed by assault guns on their own. On the 4th Division front the attack by 19th NZ Armoured Regiment and two battalions was postponed a number of times and was not launched until 6.30pm. Some progress was made, however. In the falling light the tanks and infantry had problems linking up and only achieved this two hours later when total darkness descended on the valley.

On the 17th, while the Canadians tried to extend their line beyond Pignataro, the British began to swivel around to face Monte Cassino itself. Leading elements of 78th Division swung to the north. Moving ahead of the London Irish Rifles in their drive towards Piumarola was A Squadron of the Lothians and Border Horse. About 800 yards short of the village they spotted an 88mm anti-tank gun, which they quickly disposed of. Shortly afterwards Sergeant Burns' tank was knocked out by an anti-tank gun in the village itself, after which a PzKpfw IV hove into sight, only to find itself on the receiving end of every tank in the squadron. It did not survive for long. The squadron, now reduced to eight tanks, pushed on to the crest of a heavily wooded hill and, on cresting a track on the summit, ran into another PzKpfw IV on the other side. Lieutenant Crichton's 1 Troop advanced on the enemy tank, with 3 Troop on its right and 2 Troop to the left. Though Crichton knocked out the tank, Corporal Hackett's tank from 3 Troop was knocked out and Hackett killed. The infantry then continued their advance without the tanks until evening when they reached a cluster of farm buildings and called again upon A Squadron to support their attack. By now caution had set in among the tank crews and when they crossed the track they opened up with their main guns and machine guns. Under this weight of fire the infantry literally walked into their objective, fifty German prisoners being taken and another fifty killed. In return the squadron lost one tank to a panzeschreck at short range. Over to their right 17th/21st Lancers set off towards Route 6 under a rolling barrage, encountering very little opposition as they advanced. Where they did it was in one or two farmhouses along the way and these were easily dealt with. By evening they had closed to within a few hundred metres of Route 6 and here they halted for the night. Though the infantry did send patrols across the road, no attempt was made to cross the road because of their uncertainty as to the location of the Poles.

Over to their right 4th Division, with 19th NZ Armoured Regiment in support, wheeled around and struck out for Route 6 at 7.15am. They too met little opposition and eventually cut the road less than 3km from Cassino township. Later that evening support weapons were brought up and the position consolidated. On 18 May C Squadron 19th Armoured Regiment, along with 2nd Duke of Cornwall's Light Infantry and 1st Battalion 6th East Surrey Regiment drove into Cassino, reaching the Hotel des Roses around the time the Polish flag went up over the monastery.

Though this Polish-operated Carrier tank with its Bailey bridge is not the one used by Captain Tony Kingsmill to launch 'Plymouth' bridge, it does demonstrate the principle of the system. (Zbigniew Lalak)

A Churchill Mk III from I Troop A Squadron, 51st Royal Tank Regiment moves up to join up with Canadian infantry on 17 May. (IWM)

One of the victims of 4th Division's assault on 12 May was this StuG III, most probably from StuG-Abt 242. (Shirley Hodson)

Additional support for 4th Division arrived on 15 May in the form of 19th NZ Armoured Regiment, among them Ken Brown's tank from Headquarters Troop, C Squadron. (Stuart Wilson)

This StuG III from Sturmgeschütz-Brigade 907 was knocked out near Pignataro on 15 May. (National Archives of Canada)

Lieutenant Don Kerr's tank from C Squadron of 19th NZ Armoured Regiment on reaching the Hotel des Roses on 18 May after entering Cassino. (Frank Harvey)

This aerial photograph of Cassino township shows the destruction wrought by the bombing and subsequent fighting in and around the Convent and Botanical Gardens. Note the abandoned tanks around the Convent in the foreground. (ATL)

18 May. The crew of a Sherman III rest outside their tank near the Cassino Jail for the first time. (Frank Bulling)

This Sherman III from 18th NZ Armoured Regiment passes through Cassino on 18 May on its way to join up with 8th Indian Division. (ATL)

The following three images show StuG IVs from Panzer-Abteilung 190, 90 Panzergrenadier-Division which were knocked out on 18 May near a blown bridge over the Liri River between Pontecorvo and Pignataro. (National Archives of Canada)

Chapter Eleven

Diadem – Monte Cassino

With the British and Indian troops in the Liri Valley focused on breaking the deadlock there, the Poles had the unenviable task of throwing the paratroopers off Monte Cassino. Their plan of attack called for 5th Kresowa Division to capture Phantom Ridge and Colle Sant'Angelo, while, to their left, 3th Carpathian Division were to secure Point 593 and Point 569 on Snakeshead Ridge. In between them 4th Armoured Regiment 'Skorpion' was to drive up the valley from Madras Circus, 2 Squadron supporting the Carpathians and 3 Squadron supporting the Kresowans.

The attack was launched on the night of 11/12 May after a preliminary bombardment and initially achieved some degree of success. Though the lead battalions of 5th Kresowa Division became disorganized and lost all communication back to their brigade headquarters, they did manage to clear some pillboxes despite the murderous artillery and mortar fire they were subjected to. In the end they got to onto the top of Phantom Ridge and thence to a saddle between Colle Sant'Angelo and Point 706 but were soon forced back to Phantom Ridge. There Germans tried to dislodge them in a counter-attack early the following morning but were thrown back. Other troops lower down also managed to get beyond Point 706 but, with casualties mounting under withering defensive fire, were also forced back to Point 706.

Simultaneously with this the Carpathians launched their attack on Point 593 but deprived of their armoured support were forced to go in alone. After the preliminary artillery bombardment they set off but became frustrated in their attempts to take Point 593 when they ran up against a belt of barbed wire and an extensive minefield and were forced to go to ground. Around dawn the Germans launched a counter-attack and though they were beaten off the Polish losses were so heavy that they were forced to withdraw.

The tanks supporting the Kresowans ran into problems early on. After setting off from Caira on the night of 11/12 May 1st Platoon from 3 Squadron, under the command of 2nd Lieutenant Tadeusz Trejdosiewicz, drove up Cavendish road, reaching a position close to Phantom Ridge some three hours later. There the lead tank missed the narrow track and slipped into a crater. The tank behind it was immobilised by an artillery round striking its engine compartment. When Trejdosiewicz tried to drive past this tank, his tank struck a mine that blew off its tracks. Two M10 tank destroyers that were with them then sought shelter behind a large rock and covered the crews as they abandoned their tanks, then they all withdrew to Madras Circus.

Next up Cavendish Road was 4th Platoon, 3 Squadron under 2nd Lieutenant Ludomil Bialecki, along with two other tanks from their squadron headquarters and the whole of 2 Squadron under the command of Captain Drelicharz. They were delayed in this move when the lead tank took a bend in the road at speed and ended up partially hung over the edge of a precipice, blocking further progress. An attempt was made to rescue the tank but after two fruitless hours they were forced to push it over the edge, as a result they did not reach Madras Circus until late the afternoon. Bialecki's platoon then set off towards Phantom Ridge accompanied by Captain Dzieciolowski's tank. Below the saddle between Point 593 and Phantom Ridge Bialecki's tank ran onto a mine, setting of an internal explosion that killed three of the crew and severely burned him and Corporal Josef Nikowski. Bialeki died a few minutes later but Nikowski lived for another seven days. Thus blocked, the three tanks remained there for time, providing fire support to cover the withdrawal of the Kresowans and then withdrew to Madras Circus.

The failure of this attack led a rethink by Leese. Anders's intention was to postpone their next attempt by twenty-four hours but sometime later Leese decided to delay it by a further 24 hours to allow XIII Corps to reach Route 6 in the Liri Valley. In the end, the attack did not resume until the morning of 17 May. In actual fact it was renewed much earlier than planned after a battalion from 5th Kresowa Division captured some German outposts on Phantom Ridge on the night of 16/17 May. Emboldened by this success they sent up the rest of the Battalion and by 11am were firmly established on the ridge. The division then launched an attack from Point 706 and by midmorning had cleared the north-eastern slopes of Colle Sant'Angelo. The Germans responded with a series of counter-attacks and eventually forced the Poles to withdraw to the base of the southern summit, though not for long. Reinforced by another battalion the Poles renewed their assault and by 6.00pm were firmly in control of the higher of the two peaks.

The Carpathians had less success in their attack on Point 593 and Point 569. At 9.30am they launched the first of several attacks on both peaks and while they did manage to gain a foothold on the northern part of Point 569 were soon driven off. Despite repeated attacks thereafter on Point 593 they were beaten back by the paratroopers and late that afternoon were forced to go over to the defensive.

Around 7.00am 2 Squadron set off up the valley with a battalion of Carpathian infantry and engineers. Good progress was made until they reached the second

Bottleneck. At this point the engineers were forced to retreat under heavy mortar fire, until two tanks from 4th Platoon, commanded by 2nd Lieutenant Antoni Pilatowicz and Corporal Szablowski moved up in front of them and put down a barrage of fire. With the mines thus cleared the force was able to move forward again reaching the saddle overlooking Massa Albaneta around 9.30am. There they proceeded to open up on German positions around Albaneta and Point 593, forcing the Germans out of their positions on the slopes. This prompted a small detachment of Germans to attack the Polish force with a panzerschreck but the rocket harmlessly struck the spare track links and sandbags on the glacis plate of one of the tanks. When 4th Platoon's ammunition was spent they pulled out and were replaced by 2nd Platoon under 2nd Lieutenant Hopko. By now the Poles were in a bit of a quandary. They were anxious to continue the advance down towards Massa Albaneta but the mines on the track would have to be cleared while still under fire. If they remained and continued to they would soon run out of ammunition at their present rate of fire. The matter was soon decided when another panzerschreck rocket blew the right track off one tank, killing the spare driver and forcing its crew to abandoned it. This prompted the crews of some of the other tanks to transfer ammunition from it to their tanks but had to stop when they were hit by shrapnel from artillery fire. Shortly afterwards an artillery shell landed near another Sherman, damaging its water pump, radiator and electrical system.

Around 3.00pm their platoon was withdrawn and replaced by 2nd Lieutenant Bialkowski's platoon and Lieutenant Budzianowski's tank. Some Polish infantry then started to work their way forward towards Massa Albaneta under the tanks' covering fire. The Germans responded by subjecting the tanks to a strong artillery barrage one round hitting the turret roof of Bialkowski's tank, cracking the armour and knocking out its electrical system. A small group of Germans then appeared under a Red Cross flag and surrendered. The Poles made a further attempt to move forward but soon came to a halt when they spotted mines. Their engineers came forward to clear them but when all of them were wounded this attempt was abandoned. By 7.00pm when the squadron was down to only four serviceable tanks, only one still capable of firing, they withdrew from the saddle.

Over to their right 3 Squadron launched their attack on Phantom Ridge. Covered by the tanks, the engineers proceeded to clear the mines on their way forward but when it appeared to be proceeding too slowly, 2nd Lieutenant Jan Kochanowski from 3rd Platoon sought out a way up in his tank. On his first attempt he failed, the road up the ridge being blocked by mines and large rocks. His company commander, Captain Dzieciolowski, was about to withdraw when Kochanowski tried again, this time successfully. Once on Phantom Ridge he proceeded to put down fire on the Germans, destroying two bunkers and forcing them to abandon others. His tank soon became a focal point for some German prisoners who had surrendered to the infantry earlier. These he sent down to the troops below but he was unable to cope when some more arrived and ordered them to remain in their positions. Dzieciolowski sent the rest of 3rd Platoon's tanks up the ridge, while the tanks of 2rd Platoon provided fire support from the road. Once up there they were ordered to advance on Point 575 but the best they could do was hold their position. By 4.30pm they were out of ammunition and requested permission to withdraw, which was finally given two hours later.

At dawn the following morning the tanks headed back up the valley. On climbing up to the saddle overlooking Massa Albaneta the leading tank of 3rd Platoon, 2 Squadron, under the command of Sergeant-Major Jan Mackowiak, ran onto a mine laid by the Germans inside the taped path marked by the engineers the previous day. Undeterred by this 2nd Lieutenant Jerzy Matykiewicz tried to push past it but ran onto another mine also losing a track. The engineers then moved on and began clearing mines on the track on the forward slope, while the two disabled tanks kept up a barrage of fire on Point 593. This done, the Carpathian infantry and the rest of 2 Squadron advanced down the road and secured Massa Albaneta, while some of the tanks proceeded to a point where they could fire on the monastery itself, though it was too late. As they were to soon learn 1 Fallschirmjäger-Division, under orders, had abandoned their positions the previous night, leaving on three men on Point 593 and some wounded in the monastery. The latter were discovered by a patrol from 10th Podolski Lancers when they entered the monastery around 10.20am and raised their flag over it ten minutes later.

A Sherman III from 4th Armoured Regiment 'Skorpion' carries engineers out of Cavendish Road into Madras Circus. (Zbigniew Lalak)

The Poles took over three Sherman IIIs of C Squadron, 20th NZ Armoured Regiment. They were placed under the command of Lieutenant Tadeusz Bobak. This one was based in Madras Circus. (PISM)

Unsuitable now for its primary purpose, the heavily-sandbagged Valentine bridgelayer tank behind Bobak's tank was set up to provide a shelter in their regimental headquarters and first aid post area. (PISM)

This Sherman III at the entrance to Madras Circus was also one of the New Zealand tanks taken over by the Poles and put under the command of Bobak. (Zbigniew Lalak)

During the night attack on 11/12 May 2nd Lieutenant Tadeusz Trejdosiewicz's Sherman III from 1st Platoon, 3 Squadron, slipped into this ditch. (PISM)

Shermans from 4th Armoured Regiment 'Skorpion' moving up towards the Bottleneck and the saddle overlooking Massa Albaneta. (Zbigniew Lalak)

These four images show Lieutenant Lodmir Bialecki's Sherman III from 4th Platoon, 3 Squadron which ran onto a double or triple Teller mine below the 'Bottleneck' on 12 May and was destroyed. All the crew were killed or died later. (PISM)

Second Lieutenant Białkiewicza's Sherman III from 2 Squadron carrying engineers up on the **engine** deck of his Sherman III, 'Pięść' during the attack on 17 May. (Zbigniew Lalak)

Lieutenant Edward Budzianowskiego from Regimental Headquarters took some infantry forward on his Sherman III. (Zbigniew Lalak)

One of the Polish Sherman IIIs under fire in the vicinity of the second Bottleneck and the saddle between Point 593 and Phantom Ridge. (Zbigniew Lalak)

These four images show that after reaching the saddle overlooking Massa Albaneta on 18 May the 3rd Platoon Sherman IIIs of 2 Squadron ran onto mines; Sergeant-Major Jan Mackowiak's tank on the left and 2nd Lieutenant Jerzy Matykiewicz's on the right. (PISM; NARA; Zbigniew Lalak)

On 18 May 2nd Lieutenant Jan Kochanowski from 3rd Platoon, 3 Squadron drove back up onto Phantom Ridge but this time while crossing a 45-degree slope the tank rolled down the hill and onto its turret. (PISM)

At the end of the fighting on 18 May numerous other tanks from 4th Armoured Regiment 'Skorpion' littered the battlefield, including the other ex-New Zealand Sherman III from Bobak's platoon. (PISM)

This Sherman III appears to be a marked-off area suggesting an area not cleared of mines. (PISM)

This M4A2 Sherman III in the vicinity of the Bottleneck was knocked out by an armour-piercing round that penetrated the glacis plate. (PISM)

One of the Shermans from 3 Squadron after the battle. (PISM)

A crewman effecting repairs to his Sherman III after the battle. (PISM)

Epilogue

Though the breakthrough along the Gustav Line from Cassino to the sea had been a major victory for the Allies, there was still some hard fighting to go before they could link up with the embattled troops at Anzio. Ahead of them in the Liri Valley lay the Hitler Line, which Hitler had recently renamed the Senger Line. Here the Germans had set up a complex system of anti-tank ditches, barbed wire and minefields covered by anti-tank guns and dug-in turrets to strengthen what was not a natural defensive position. Potentially a formidable obstacle, particularly with the use of Panther turrets, the problem for the Germans was this line was not quite complete when the Allies turned their attention to it. Nevertheless, it could not be overcome without some difficulty and it was not till 25 May that the Allies finally broke through and were in a position to link up with their fellows at Anzio.

Thus after four months the Allies had finally achieved what they set out to do, break through to Rome on what they had considered the easy route of the Liri Valley. The questions are was it worth it and was there a better way. Early on in the fighting the CEF commander, General Juin, had proposed a wider flanking movement involving an advance through the mountain pass to the north of Cassino via Atina towards Sora. As had been demonstrated by the capture of Monte Maio by the French in May 1944, such a move could have achieved the same thing without the heavy losses experienced both in among the fighting troops and the civilian population. The destruction of the town of Cassino and the monastery might have been avoided. But that, of course, did not happen.

So how did armour fare in the battle for Cassino and was it of much use? One thing which was apparent was the vastly different environments under which the armoured troops found themselves operating in around the town. In the case of the fighting in Cassino itself there were unique difficulties associated with the town prior to the bombing and after it. Certainly armoured troops are never happy in built-up areas even when infantry are working in close support, a view expressed even by Edwin Metzger, whose platoon of assault guns was based within Cassino during the early American attacks. Once Allied armour was confined to the narrow streets of the towns in Italy there were always good opportunities for ambushes by determined infantry equipped with weapons such as the panzerscheck and panzerfaust. Opposing armour could also dominate the streets simply by virtue of their having the first aimed shot at any tank that happened to poke its nose around the corner. This is something the Americans experienced when they first entered Cassino in February, a well-positioned assault gun taking out three Shermans in as many minutes, thus breaking up the American attack on the Jail before it even got going.

When the issue of bombing the town was discussed Freyberg was dismissive of the view put forward by others that it would be impossible for his tanks to get into the town. He responded by saying that the Germans would also have difficulties; something that proved to be true. The problem was that, though the bombing eliminated two of the assault guns in the middle of the town, the one that did survive, along with a PzKpfw IV, was of considerable value in blocking the New Zealander's attempts to clear the area around the Hotel Continental. Nevertheless those New Zealand tanks that made it into Cassino did provide good support for the infantry there and were critical in the capture of the railway station.

One area where the employment of tanks seemed less likely was on the Cassino massif and it only came about as an afterthought. Even then it was only regarded as a secondary operation to the main attack on the monastery, only becoming the main attack when the other collapsed in the face of the German attack on Castle Hill. That the Cavendish Road attack failed after having achieved so much could be put down to their inability to obtain infantry support but this may be a somewhat simplistic viewpoint. After the battle the Poles came to the view that the individual thrusts along Snakeshead Ridge, Phantom Ridge and in the valley between them were bound to fail. Instead they felt that attack would only succeed if all three attacks were launched simultaneously, something that was not possible during the Third Battle of Cassino thanks to the losses suffered by 4th Indian Division earlier. This was because the Poles saw Points 593 and 569 as being at the centre of interlocking fields of fire ranging from the monastery to Phantom Ridge, Colle Sant'Angelo and Massa Albaneta. Attacking just one of these positions allowed the Germans to concentrate their fire on the assault troops, while their fire would be more diluted in dealing with a thrust on a broader front.

While not detracting from the capture of Monte Maio by the French, which was really the key to unlocking the Gustav Line, there was still the need to make progress in the Liri and Ausente Valleys. In the case of the latter, at least, the Americans had the advantage of holding positions on the western side of the Garigliano River. The British on the other hand still had to cross theirs but, learnt the lessons of the Texans and paid particular attention to getting bridges over the Gari River as soon as possible. To that end they were even willing to countenance the innovative approach of Tony Kingsmill in using two Sherman tanks to launch a fully-assembled Bailey bridge. In that their gamble paid off, even if only four tanks made it across initially. Certainly the critical difference between the assaults by 8th Indian Division and 4th Division was the tank support that the former received early on in the battle. With this support the Indians were able to enlarge their bridgehead on the first day, while troops from one brigade from 4th Division were left clinging to a very narrow bridgehead until they could complete Amazon Bridge.

Thus it would seem that, though some of the areas around Cassino were not ideal for the operation of armour it nevertheless played an important role in the unlocking of the Gustav Line.

A heavily-weathered Sherman in Cassino exhibits two armour-piercing strikes on its turret, one of which has penetrated the tank on the turret ring. (NARA)

Indian troops inspect an abandoned Sherman III from 5 Troop, B Squadron, 19th NZ Armoured Regiment. (NARA)

With the battle over work began on clearing Cassino township, engineers here clearing rubble in the town in the shadow of a knocked-out Sherman. (NARA)

New Zealand engineers in the process of pulling a Sherman III out of a crater. (George Andrews)

This is presumably one of the Valentine bridgelayer tanks seen drowned in a crater along Route 6. (George Andrews)

Tanks that could not be repaired, like this Sherman, were cut up for scrap. (NARA)

Left and above: Schumann's StuG III was found in the rubble of the Palazzon Iucci. After he and his crew had been relieved, their assault gun gradually became hemmed in by rubble from the constant bombardment to the point where it could no longer venture out of its garage so its crew blew it up. (NARA)

This StuG III remained a little longer outside the Chiesa di San Antonio. After the local Italians stripped it of its tracks and running gear they used it to tie their cattle up to. (PISM)

With Cassino cleared of the Germans and the railway embankment repaired, the Americans were able to start shuttling their tanks forward along it. (NARA)

Only one tank that took part in the battle for Cassino remained in the area after the war. The Poles decided to turn Bialecki's M4A2 Sherman into a monument. Here they are at work on the construction of the cross from Sherman tracks. (PISM)

The completed Polish monument. (PISM)

Bibliography

Dawson, W.D., *18th Battalion and Armoured Regiment* (War History Branch, Department of Internal Affairs, Wellington, 1961)

Fazedin, R., *The 756th Tank Battalion in the Battle of Cassino* (iUniverse, Lincoln, NE, 1991)

Krebs, J.E., and Froeschle, H.O., *To Rome and Beyond: With Our Story of the 760th Tank Battalion, WWII* (Traffiord, Bloomington, 2007)

Lalak, Z., *Pulk Pancerny 'Skorpion'. 4th Armoured Regiment 'Scorpion'* (Pegaz-Bis, Warsaw, 2003)

Molony, Brigadier C.J.C., *The Mediterranean and the Middle East, Volume VI, Part 1, British Official History of the Second World War* (HMSO, London, 1984)

Phillips, C., *Italy. Volume I. The Sangro to Cassino* (War History Branch, Department of Internal Affairs, Wellington, 1957)

Plowman, J., *Rampant Dragons. New Zealanders in Armour in World War II* (Kiwi Armour, Christchurch 2002)

Plowman, J., and Perry R., *The Battles for Monte Cassino Then and Now* (Battle of Britain International, Old Harrow, 2011)

Pringle, D.J.C., and Glue, W.A., *20th Battalion and Armoured Regiment* (War History Branch, Department of Internal Affairs, Wellington, 1957)

Sinclair, D.W., *19th Battalion and Armoured Regiment* (War History Branch, Department of Internal Affairs, Wellington, 1954)

Zuehlke, M., *The Liri Valley. Canada's WWII Breakthrough to Rome* (Douglas McIntyre, Vancouver, 2001)